FAT FREE

FAT FREE
COMMON SENSE FOR
YOUNG WEIGHT WORRIERS
BY SARA GILBERT

COLLIER BOOKS

A Division of
MACMILLAN PUBLISHING CO., INC.
New York
COLLIER MACMILLAN PUBLISHERS
London

NOTE TO READERS: Before beginning any diet, you should consult either your family doctor or a medical clinic so that you can select the diet that is right for you.

Special thanks are due to Dr. Fredda Ginsberg and Dr. Henry Berman, pediatricians and obesity specialists at The Mt. Sinai Hospital in New York City, for sharing their time and expertise.

Fat Free is published in a hardcover edition by Macmillan Publishing Co., Inc.
Printed in the United States of America
First Collier Books edition 1978

LIBRARY OF CONGRESS CATALOGING IN PUBLICATION DATA
Gilbert, Sara D. Fat free. Bibliography: p. Includes index.
SUMMARY: Discusses some social, psychological, and physiological reasons why people get fat, examines some popular diets, and advises young adults on losing weight.
1. Obesity in children—Juvenile literature. 2. Reducing—Juvenile literature. [1. Weight control] I. Title.
[RJ399.C6G54 1978] 613.2'5 77–16186 ISBN 0–02–043250–X

For Fatso

INTRODUCTION

When high school students are asked to list the medical and personal problems that bother them, concern about weight is the problem most frequently noted. It is also one of the most serious medical problems that I see in my teen-age patients. Most important, excessive weight gain during adolescence can be a major cause of adult obesity, for the following reason. It has been proved that a fat child has many more fat cells in his or her body than a child of normal weight. Once these extra cells are produced, they are never lost, and these extra fat cells lead to a lifelong problem in weight control. It also seems that another crucial period is early adolescence—a large weight gain at this age can lead to a permanent increase in the number of fat cells, and to a subsequent adult weight problem.

Fat Free is directed to those who can benefit most from it—teen-agers. A successful effort at weight control during these years can minimize the likelihood of a serious weight problem during adulthood. In addition, this book studiously avoids announcing yet another simple cure-all for the problem. Rather, it emphasizes the complexity of dealing with adolescent overweight and the difficulties in achieving weight control. *Fat Free* is therefore a very honest book; any doctor or patient who has struggled with overweight knows there is no easy way to lose weight and keep it off.

Fat Free also contains scientific information that helps explain what fat is and where it comes from; in addition, the dieting and exercise charts and the annotated bibliography are most helpful. I think the Food Intake Chart at the beginning of Chapter 7 is especially ingenious. It clarifies the relationship between the food eaten and the circumstances under which it was eaten. An understanding of this relationship is essential to a successful program of weight control.

This book is not written for those who are looking for a magical solution. As Dorothy learns in the movie of *The Wizard of Oz*, the solution to your problems can only be found within yourself. I hope *Fat Free* can provide the information and the impetus to help teen-agers find that solution.

Henry S. Berman, M.D.
Director of Health Services
The State University of New York at Stony Brook

CONTENTS

FAT FREE

ONE
NAME-CALLING

Think of all the names that tease and hurt an over-weight person.

Fatso. Fatty. Fats. Porky. Jellybelly. Lardo. Chubs. Flabbo. Tubby. Dumbo. Tubs. Blimp. Blimpy. Hippy the Hippo.

You can probably think of more. You may have been called some of those names. You may have used them on someone else. Right here on the page, in a list, they may make you want to laugh. But when they are used on you, they probably aren't so funny. They can make a person feel angry, lonely, and hopeless, all at the same time.

Of course, it isn't the teasing that's the problem. It's the fat. Even more than the fat, it's the way you *feel* about the fat and about yourself. Halfway through junior high school, I remember, lots of kids I knew started worrying about being "fat." Since I'd been fat for as long as I could remember, I thought my friends were kidding when they moaned about their "flab" or their "pot bellies." But they weren't.

For some of them, even the slender ones, just worrying about being tubby really became a problem. They convinced themselves that they were fat, and therefore ugly. They thought poorly of themselves, and this affected everything they tried to do.

It's too bad that when you first begin to pay attention to your body, usually about junior-high-school time, your body is doing such strange things. It may have become a little pudgy. It may be out of proportion. But that is because your body is changing so fast. And if you crawl into a hole marked "fat and ugly" you can harm yourself badly.

Few grown-ups who think about it would ever tease a child or a teen-ager. They frown and shake their heads about how "cruel" children can be when they tease. But they can say cruel things too, perhaps without meaning to. They may not call a kid "fatty," but they use words that make you feel at least as embarrassed and uncomfortable.

"Oh, Tommy's such a roly-poly butterball!"

"Yessir, a real heavyweight!"

"You aren't fat. You're just plump!" Or "chunky," "stocky," "chubby," "pudgy," "heavy."

"Just wait, all that will turn into muscle!"

"Sally eats so much because she's a growing girl."

"That? That's just baby fat. You'll grow out of it."

"That little roll around your tummy? It's just a stage you're going through."

Now, maybe your parents, your teachers, or your doctors are right—and maybe they aren't—when they say those things. If they are, and you can talk to them about it, they should be able to give you a careful explanation of why what you think is fat is really just a "stage" or a "stocky bone structure." But if you aren't just "plump" or "growing"—if you *are* fat, and you feel it and know it, all those "polite" words only make you feel worse.

Maybe you have been fat since you were a baby, or maybe you've just added a layer of fat recently. You may be carrying around ten or fifteen extra pounds—maybe much more. Whatever your condition, if adults are so embarrassed about your weight that they have to call it "plump" or "muscle," then you might think being fat must be something to be ashamed of. If the body you walk around in all day seems so shameful to others you might even begin to believe that the person inside that body is no good. And that is just not true.

Let's be honest in this book. Kids may chant mean words. Parents may use polite words. Doctors may make fine distinctions between terms like "obesity" and "overweight." Here, we're just going to talk about *fat*.

Say it out loud—"fat." It's not such a bad word by itself. But our knowledge about fat is fuzzy. Our attitudes toward fat are confused. We get embarrassed to even say the word.

You may say "I'm fat" and mean you're really obese—more than 30 percent above the average weight for your height and age. You may say "I'm fat" and mean you're overweight, by a lot, or a little. Or you may say "I'm fat" and mean you just *feel* fatter than you want to feel.

What is fat and how do you feel about it? If you are worried about being fat, you should know right now that:

. . . you may not be fat, no matter how fat you feel;

. . . even if you are fat, you have nothing to be ashamed of;

. . . you aren't the only one—an estimated one-fifth of all school-age children are too fat;

. . . fat is a complicated problem that you should not have to solve alone;

. . . you *can* do something about it.

TWO
A GOOD HARD LOOK

This book is going to ask you to take a good hard look at yourself. You can begin by looking in a mirror. Find one that will show all or almost all of you, in good light and in some privacy. If there isn't a full-length mirror around your house, you can get one at a dime store or hardware store for just a few dollars, and attach it to a door in your room or in the bathroom. Or maybe there's a good mirror in the gym at school.

When you look, what do you see?

BABY FAT?

Stand sideways. Can you see your ribs? Your jaw line? Are you generally flat, front and back, and from top to bottom? Or are you pear-shaped? If you look round and padded instead of straight and bony, don't run and hide—look again.

A boy who hasn't started to broaden through the chest and shoulders, or a girl who hasn't widened a bit at the hips and narrowed at the waist may still have a little-kid's body. If all you see is a padded tummy, chipmunk cheeks, and a soft behind—it's probably just baby fat.

Most babies look like half-inflated beachballs. Even if they aren't overweight, they may have chubby arms and legs, round, soft chins and cheeks, and bulging bellies. By the time kids start kindergarten, most of them have lost this first layer of fat. They are longer and leaner in the legs and the midsection. Then, around the time of second grade, many kids get pudgy again, and they may not start thinning out until their bodies are almost full-grown.

You probably haven't noticed your changing size and shape until now. For the first time, you may be aware of your appearance. Maybe you see your friends and classmates getting tall and looking grown-up, and you stare at your reflection and see only a pudgy ball. It can be discouraging. But unless you've had a weight problem throughout your life, you're still in the "baby fat" stage.

"But how can it be baby fat? I don't feel like a baby. I'm *not* a baby!" Of course you're not. Between the ages of about ten and twelve people begin to grow out of childhood and toward adulthood. But emotional growth and physical growth don't always happen at the same time. Some children take on the shapes of adult men and women while they still feel and act like what they are inside—children. Other people are "grown-ups" inside long before they stop looking like children. So no matter how old you feel, your body can still be that of a child.

If you don't yet have any noticeable body hair, if your friends have started growing taller than you, and if your shape is more like your younger brother's or sister's than like your parents', a slight padding is perfectly normal.

It is as though your body were storing up extra supplies before the big growth spurt that follows the rather slow development between ages seven and ten. You *will* start growing—and fast. Maybe not tomorrow or next week, but in a few months or a year you'll be into the period of maximum growth when boys and girls gain height and weight with incredible speed. According to national surveys, girls between ages ten and sixteen gain about fifty pounds and add about nine inches; boys between twelve and eighteen gain some sixty pounds and ten inches. These added dimensions show up in new shapes, as little-kid bulges turn into adult curves.

Your friends may have already entered this high-growth stage. Different people grow at different paces, and you will catch up. So try to be patient, and don't eat yourself into real fat while worrying about baby fat.

OR PUPPY FAT?

"Yeah, but what about *me?*" a twelve-year-old girl protests. "I'm as tall as my friends, taller than some, and my shape is getting to look more like my mother's than my kid sister's. I've never been too heavy in my life, but now, when it *counts*, I'm fat!"

Your reflection in the mirror may show that you are definitely not a baby any more. You may be sprouting body hair. You may be able to see where your waist belongs. Girls can see signs of breasts; boys notice changes in their genitals. Extra fat may still be normal.

Many girls at about eleven, and boys at about twelve or thirteen, enter the "puppy fat" stage. Even girls who have always been skinny will gain a layer of soft fat—especially around the waist, hips, and thighs—and a rounded abdomen. They will lose some of this pudge by adulthood, but probably not all of it. Females tend to be softer—"fatter"—than males. Boys entering adolescence may acquire patches of fat on their upper thighs, their abdomens, and around their nipples. Most grow out of it by age eighteen.

Puppy fat, annoying as it may be, is actually a good sign. It shows that your body is working hard to leave childhood and mature. Your glands, or regulatory organs, are beginning to manufacture new hormones that stimulate growth and activate the reproductive system. Various glands produce hormones from birth (and perhaps even before). These substances flow through our bodies, controlling growth and other physical functions. But at puberty, the time when girls start to menstruate and boys begin to mature sexually, new hormones are needed. Some signs that these new "juices" are flowing are face and body hair and the coarse, oily skin that sometimes results in acne. Temporary extra body fat is one side effect of new hormonal production.

At puberty, not only does your body get fatter for a while, but it gets heavier, too. Your bones take on more heft; your frame broadens. A boy's shoulders widen. A girl's pelvis shifts position to make room for developing reproductive organs. This shifting can cause a "pot belly" young teen-age girls abhor.

Puppy fat and the sudden increase in your weight can be alarming. But you will grow through this awkward stage. Just hearing that may not be very comforting, but it is important that you believe it. Your parents, your teachers, your doctor, your older brothers and sisters—every adult has gone through this worrisome period. It can be a painful time. But if you let worries over your appearance get you down, you can make growing up harder than it has to be.

Researchers at a New York hospital found that only 15 percent of the teen-age girls they studied were actually fat, but 50 percent *thought* they were fat and were worried about it. So don't be too critical of that reflection in your mirror. Be honest. If the fat is new, and not extreme, try to forget about it and keep busy doing the things that make you happy.

OR JUST PLAIN FAT?

Okay, some fat is normal. But you may be one of those people for whom "baby fat" and "puppy fat" are just excuses. If you have been overweight for a long time—much heavier than your classmates, heavy enough for the doctor to comment on—or if you have gained a lot of weight without growing much taller in the last year or two, then take a harder look at that reflection.

Don't pull in your stomach or tighten your muscles. Just stand normally and look. Is it impossible to see whatever waist you have? Are your ribs hidden under a layer of flesh? Has your original chin disappeared? Do you have rolls and creases in your front and dimples and wrinkles on your backside?

You can also measure yourself for excess fat. First, pinch yourself: with your thumb and forefinger, pick up a fold of flesh on the back of your upper arm; then at the bottom of your rib cage; and then, if possible, on your back, just below your shoulder blade. If the flesh between your fingers is about an inch wide, you have too much body fat. The wider the fold, the fatter you are.

To double check, find a ruler. Lie down on your back on a flat surface, without stretching out or sucking in your stomach. Place the ruler lengthwise across your abdomen, with one end on your rib cage and the other on your pelvic bone, as though it were a bridge on the route from your shoulder to your knee. If the ruler touches both your ribs and your pelvis, you may not have a real fat problem. But if you have a bulge in your midriff big enough to hold the ruler away from one bone or another, you are too fat. It may help you to know that 40 percent of all Americans "fail" this ruler test.

Why don't we just tell you to get on the scales and compare your weight with an ideal weight on a chart? Because, these charts are based on a *statistical average* of all people in your age and height range. Depending on your bone structure and muscular development, you can be "overweight" according to many charts without being fat, and you can be "normal" or even underweight by those standards and still be carrying too much fat. You can't go by most charts for your "normal" weight because each person has his or her own "normal" weight.

Even for adults, the charts are too often inaccurate. For teen-agers, whose size, shape, and growth rates vary so sharply within their age ranges, these charts can be downright damaging and depressing. And they're beside the point. Because this book—and you—are concerned with fat, not "size." Scales will tell you how much you weigh, but the way you feel about your weight is more important.

Your doctor is the best person to make a final judgment about your weight. Besides weighing and measuring you accurately, the doctor can tell how much of your weight is fat, and how much is muscle and bone, and he can place it in the perspective of your stage of development.

No matter how you *feel*, the doctor may consider your weight to be within the "normal" range—that is, 10 percent above or below the average weight for people your age and height.

You may just be "flabby," even though your weight is exactly right. Flab, whether or not it includes excess weight, is just loose flesh. The muscles are not strong enough to hold the flesh in place. Good posture and effective exercise can strengthen the muscles and get you back in shape.

You may be "padded" with an extra five or ten pounds. Although this weight might fall within the "normal" range for your height and age, the few excess pounds may make you feel uncomfortable and unattractive. You probably want to get your weight down to the point at which you feel happy with yourself.

You may be "overweight." If you weigh from 10 to 20 percent more than you should, you are slightly overweight. If you are 20 to 30 percent above the average, your overweight is more severe. Countless numbers of people fall into the "overweight" group. And since weight tends to increase throughout adulthood, the earlier you can take off your extra pounds, the better chance you'll have for a healthy, active life.

You may be "obese." Doctors usually define obesity as weight that is 30 percent above what's average for a person's age, height, and bone structure. This means that if you should weigh 100 pounds, but you weigh 130 pounds or more, you are obese. Many Americans of all ages fall into the "obese" category, and a surprisingly large number of young people are twice or even three times as heavy as they should be. Obesity, besides being unattractive to many people, is a health hazard at any age.

Obese, overweight, or padded—whatever the word, it means too much body fat. But what exactly *is* fat?

THREE
WHAT IS FAT?

"Fat is the roll around my middle that shows even under my sweatshirt."

"Fat is the lumps on my legs that make me want to cry when I put on a bathing suit."

True. But for now try to forget how you *feel* about fat, and concentrate on fat as a fact of life. Fats are substances consisting primarily of complex chains of carbon, hydrogen and oxygen atoms. The scientific word for fat is "lipid," and it exists in several forms, including esters, triglycerides, fatty acids and phosphatides.

Body fat (the kind we're concerned with) is similar to raw chicken fat—translucent, yellow and somewhat greasy. Stored in special cells, called adipose cells, beneath the skin and around the vital organs, it serves to cushion the organs and bones and to provide insulation against the cold. Fat cells occur throughout the body, but they are concentrated in the buttocks, the abdomen, the upper arms and thighs, and sometimes the cheeks and chin. The exact reason for these points of concentration is not known. An excess of body fat can mean you have too many fat cells, too much fat in existing cells, or both.

The body stores fat in order to provide energy for future use. Energy is "the ability to do work." Work may mean mowing the lawn or rocketing to the moon. Your body needs energy to do the work of growing, repairing itself and keeping you active. For every eye blink and heartbeat, for every bit of food you digest, for every one of the countless cells your body replaces daily, you use energy.

THE ENERGY BANK

You get energy from the foods you eat. Your body converts food into heat energy to maintain temperature levels and to power activities, and into chemical energy for repair, maintenance, and storage. We speak of "burning" food or energy, though "burn" is just shorthand for a complex series of chemical changes. The processes by which foods are converted into energy are called digestion, respiration absorption, and metabolism.

Chemically, all foods—steak or peanut butter, tuna casserole or tortillas, milkshakes or pecan pie— are simply different combinations of atoms, primarily carbon, hydrogen and oxygen, with lesser amounts of nitrogen, calcium, sulfur and phosphorus, and smaller amounts of other elements. *Any* food that is not converted into energy can be changed into fat and stored. This means that any food can be "fattening" if you eat too much of it. Celery, for instance, is thought of as a good "diet" food. But if you eat more celery than your body can use, it will be converted and stored as fat.

Though all foods are essentially the same and can all be turned into body fat, there are some basic differences among them. We eat three basic types of food: proteins, fats, and carbohydrates. The arrangements of the atoms and molecules, and the relative amounts of the elements within each molecule, differ for each type. Each category—protein, fat, and carbohydrate—has a specific assignment in the body.

Protein is the major ingredient in the walls of the body's cells—and remember, your body is really nothing more than billions of cells. You use the protein you eat to build new cells and to repair worn-out ones. Enzymes, which are chemicals that, among other things make possible the digestion of all foods, are also proteins.

You obtain proteins primarily from meat, fish, poultry, eggs, milk products, nuts, and beans. Because they are so vital to life, it is hard to take in more protein than the body can use, but it is possible.

The body uses *carbohydrates* partly to help digest

fats, but mainly as fuel to keep the system going. When cells burn carbohydrate molecules, they produce heat. Some of this heat goes to maintain body temperature, but most of it provides quick energy.

You get carbohydrates from fruits, sugars, from foods made with flour (breads, crackers, pastas), and from rice, potatoes, corn, and other vegetables. Carbohydrates are plentiful, and if you don't use all the fuel they provide, the extra is converted into fat and stored.

Fats are the easiest to store and the hardest to burn. They provide some energy for activity, but primarily they keep the body warm. To function properly, you must maintain a constant temperature within your body, and fats are the fuel that heats the system.

You eat vegetable fats—oils from seeds and plants —and animal fats, from meats, milk products, and butter. You may not take in as many fats as other foods, but fats contain more than twice the calories of carbohydrates or proteins.

COUNTING CALORIES

And what exactly is a calorie? A calorie is a way to measure heat, like a degree mark on a thermometer. Heat is one form of energy provided by food. Calories measure the amount of energy that a given food is capable of producing when it is burned by the body.

A pound of pure protein contains about 1800 calories.

A pound of pure carbohydrate contains about 1800 calories.

A pound of pure fat contains about 4000 calories.

Body fat represents stored energy. A pound of *body fat* contains 3500 calories. That's 3500 units of potential energy that need to be burned if the fat is to leave your body. Since energy is "the ability to do work," it requires work to burn the stored energy off. To change one pound of body fat into weightless energy, you must do 3500 calories' worth of work. You must force your body to burn some of its stored fat.

Reducing diets are designed to do just that. A low-calorie diet limits the number of calories you may take in, so that your body starts burning its stored calories. A low-carbohydrate diet accomplishes the same result, since you probably take in most of your excess calories in the form of carbohydrates. Some recent fad diets have combined a no-carbohydrate, high-protein pattern with a high-fat menu, on the theory that fats make you feel fuller longer. But a high-fat diet does little to encourage your body to use up its existing supplies of fat.

We'll go into the various diets in detail later. Now, let's look at the foods you eat that put that fat there in the first place.

WHERE DOES IT COME FROM?

It's summer vacation, say. You've been busy doing nothing all morning with your friends. Suddenly, you're all tired. So you stop in at the local hangout for lunch. You and your friends eat cheeseburgers, french fries, side orders of cole slaw, and chocolate shakes. Pretty soon, you feel perkier, but you grab some peanuts on the way out to save for later. Lunch has given your bodies enough fuel to keep going for the afternoon and still take care of basic maintenance.

What supplies did the lunch provide? Each part of it contained a mixture, but generally, the hamburger, melted cheese, peanuts, and the milk in the shake supplied protein.

The hamburger roll, the french fries, the cole slaw, and the peanuts are largely carbohydrates. If the flour in the roll has been artificially "enriched" at the mill, if the french fries and the cabbage were reasonably fresh, these foods—and the milk—contained important vitamins and minerals, too.

But what about the fats? There was no butter on the roll, no oil visible on the salad, no fat to be seen on the meat. But whole milk, cheese, ice cream, and chocolate are rich in fat. Peanuts are an excellent source of vegetable oil. The mayonnaise in the cole slaw dressing is made of fat-filled egg yolks and vegetable oil. The french fries were probably fried in fat, some of which they soaked up. And the hamburger meat may have contained as much as 25 percent fat.

Depending on the size of the portions and the method of cooking, that lunch probably contained anywhere from 1250 to 2000 calories. If you are in a growth spurt, and if you spend the afternoon swimming and running, you could burn those calories before supper.

But if you sunbathe lazily all afternoon, you won't burn up that lunch. It will get stored as body fat. If you spend the summer eating more than you burn, you'll go back to school a lot thicker in the waist, softer in the hips, and chubbier under the chin than when you left in June. The body simply refuses to waste any of its supplies, and any extra it gets, it stores.

HUNGRY CELLS

Some people, it seems, have less trouble adding fat (and more trouble losing it) than others. Over the years, medical science has developed various theories to explain this difference. One recent theory, which has gained wide acceptance, is that many fat people have too many fat cells. According to important research, these extra fat cells develop first in infancy and early childhood. Fat cells may also multiply in adolescence, but once growth stops, no new fat cells will be added (though a person can gain weight by adding fat to the existing cells). Once the extra cells have developed, they will not go away. Dieting and exercise can make each cell give up some of its fat and get smaller but cannot reduce the total number of cells. Not only that, but once the amount of fat in each cell drops below a certain level, the cell seems to get "greedy," and converts every bit of food it can into fat.

Researchers suspect, though they have not proved it, that a pattern resulting in excess fat cells *may* be passed from parent to child through the genes. It is also possible that women who gain too much weight during pregnancy may give birth to babies who tend to produce excess fat cells.

What *is* known for certain is that babies and small children develop too many fat cells because they eat too much. A baby is an excellent judge of how much and what it needs to eat. So how could it eat too much and produce all those unnecessary cells? Its parents feed it too much, of course. But why?

For one thing, it is only in the last few years that

these facts about early overfeeding and fat cells have been available. To many people who became parents before this was known, a fat baby was a healthy baby. Also, inexperienced parents, or parents with a lot of older children to care for, often use food— extra bottles of milk and snacks—to pacify a bored or fussy baby.

It may be, too, that some babies are hungrier than others. Researchers are finding that some people with a tendency toward fatness produce more insulin than the normal body needs. Insulin is a hormone manufactured by the pancreas. An excess of it increases the appetite and stimulates the body to store fat. Some babies are born with too much insulin, and for a few years they may continue to produce more than they need. So they are hungrier than others. They eat more, and they produce too many fat cells, which will remain with them for life.

What does this fat-cell theory mean for you? If you have been fat since you were very young, the chances are great that you are carrying around too many fat cells.

It is tempting to throw up your hands in despair and keep on eating since you "can't get slim anyway." But before you make a major raid on the refrigerator, stop and think. You *can* keep your weight down by keeping the level of fat in your fat cells to a minimum. You cannot do it by crash dieting, because as soon as you stop starving yourself, those greedy little cells are going to soak up all the extra calories your normal diet provides. You can do it instead by learning how to cook and eat the kinds of foods that will keep your mouth happy and your body healthy for a lifetime and that will keep your children from repeating your fat-cell pattern. And you can start forming the habit now of getting more exercise than the average flabby adult, so that you can burn up the calories before they're stored as fat. Lots of people have too many fat cells, but *you* can keep them under control.

If you have never had a weight problem before, but are getting fat (or worried about it) only now, you still have to watch out for fat cells. It seems that new fat cells may develop during adolescence as well as infancy. That means that if you let yourself get fat now, you may be eating yourself into a problem that won't go away.

THE BODY TRAP

Some people stay slim simply by burning more energy than others. It is obvious that a boy or girl who is headed for the Olympic swimming team and who swims miles every day can eat more food without gaining weight than a normally active teen-ager. Swimming is vigorous exercise that uses a lot of fuel.

But what about Pat and Ronnie, who live next door to each other? They are at the same age and stage of growth. They seem to eat about the same amounts of food. They play and work just about equally. But Pat doesn't have a weight problem, and Ronnie does.

It may be that Pat's *metabolism rate*—the speed and efficiency with which the body burns food—is higher than Ronnie's. Your thyroid gland, in your neck, controls the rate of metabolism. Not too long ago, many doctors thought that much overweight could be explained by an underactive or faulty thyroid gland. But after years of testing, doctors have concluded that thyroid trouble is a cause for obesity in only very rare cases. Among thin and fat people within a given age range, the rates of metabolism are remarkably similar. (A simple test can determine thyroid functioning, and before your doctor puts you on a diet, he may want to give you the test. But chances are heavily against your thyroid being the culprit in your weight problem.)

It may be that Pat's body works in a way different from Ronnie's. It may be more tense, for instance. Or Pat may simply move more in leading the same daily routine as Ronnie. People who never sit still, who constantly tap or jiggle a hand or a foot, can simply jitter away all the calories they take in.

Or, it may be that Ronnie really does eat more

than Pat, but in ways that neither one notices. An extra piece of toast at breakfast, a snack at every pass of the refrigerator, an extra spoonful of sauce on ice cream, a cookie at bedtime, even a pack of gum a day—those little invisible extras can add up to a lot of highly visible fat in very little time. *The addition of all those "little nothings" to the diet is often the reason why some people gain weight when others don't.*

FAMILY TRAITS

Some people might look at Ronnie's plump parents and at Pat's thin ones and conclude, "It's just heredity! Ronnie inherited fatness and Pat didn't."

Obesity itself cannot be passed from one generation to another. But there is loud debate among medical researchers about whether the *tendency* toward fatness, and the physical factors producing it, can be inherited. Studying adopted children, researchers have shown that some children born to obese natural parents but raised by slim adoptive parents will be fat, thus "proving" that obesity is inherited. But since this doesn't happen in every case—some children produced by fat parents but brought up by thin ones will not be overweight—fat may not be the fault of the genes.

Many doctors have noted that a fat child almost

always has at least one fat parent. Some take this as a sign that a cause of obesity is passed along in the genes. But others feel that parent and child simply share the same social or emotional causes of over-weight.

The facts do indicate that persons of certain body builds seem to gain weight more easily than others. For whatever reason, broadly-built, stocky, heavy-boned people tend more toward overweight than do tall, narrow-boned people. You *do* inherit your family's frame and bone structure. To that extent you might be able to blame your fat on your genes.

One family characteristic that does influence your weight is the pattern of eating and activity. If your family eats small, lean meals with no snacks, and goes in for a lot of vigorous exercise, you will acquire these non-fattening habits early in life. But if your family eats a lot and sits a lot and thus puts on weight, so will you.

FOUR
FEEDING THE SOCIAL ANIMAL

People are fat because they take in more fuel than they burn up. But it is not so simple. If being overweight were only a matter of overeating, then all of us could eat less and weigh less. The question is, *why* do you eat more than your body needs?

Animals in their natural habitat eat only what they need. *Did You Ever See a Fat Squirrel?* is the title of one popular diet book, and the answer is—no. Built into all animals are systems that control the intake and outgo of food energy. An animal "knows" instinctively when and how much it has to eat to stay healthy.

Some animals—snakes, for instance—gorge themselves incredibly with one big kill, and then can and do go without food for days or weeks. Others, like birds, must keep eating almost constantly in order to balance their intake and outgo. Animals that hibernate follow internal signals to stock up on fat to fuel themselves during the long winter of sleepy inactivity. Animals that live where it is very cold carry a heavy layer of fat to keep warm.

Animals in captivity get fat from lack of exercise and from the errors of their misguided owners. But no wild animal eats more than it needs. A fat rabbit, after all, would have a lot of trouble running from its enemies. A fat lion would have to work so hard running after its supper that it would be a thin lion in no time.

TAKING THE CUES

The human animal has a system of internal eating cues, too. Two different parts of your body—your stomach and your brain—give you cues about when and how much to eat. When the amount of food in your stomach falls below a certain level, you feel "hunger pangs." The sides of your stomach are *not* rubbing together. Nor does your stomach physically stretch or shrink much with overeating or dieting. Rather, hunger pangs are the "empty" signals that nerve sensors send to the brain when the stomach contains less food than it is accustomed to.

You can't feel the other cues, but they are just as important, if not more so. They come from a small but vital gland in the middle of your brain, the hypothalamus. Within the hypothalamus is an appetite control center. This "appestat" responds to changes in the chemistry of your blood. Part of it lets your system know when enough time has elapsed since the previous meal. Part of it signals when enough food has been taken in. The hypothalamus helps control how often and how much a person eats. There is evidence that damage to this tiny organ does, in some cases, upset a person's natural eating habits. Also, once a heavy-eating pattern is established, the physiological balance can be thrown off. But it is rare that overeating and overweight can be blamed on a malfunctioning hypothalamus.

The problem most fat people have, and most slim ones do not, is that they don't eat according to the internal cues from the stomach and the appestat. They eat according to *external* cues.

MAKING IT A HABIT

The human animal is the ultimate in social creatures. People eat when they are hungry, or when they need an energy boost. But more often than not we eat because something looks good; because we are feeling bored, excited, or sad; because it's "time" to eat; or because "everyone else" is eating.

Remember that cheeseburger lunch we talked about in Chapter 3? Say you'd eaten a big breakfast before going to the beach. You didn't do much swimming, and when the other kids went to the Shack for lunch, you weren't hungry at all. But it was lunch-time, and the gang was going to the Shack, so you went along too. You could have had just a diet soda, but you would have felt weird. Besides, everything smelled so good! Your body didn't need a big lunch, but your social self did.

That evening, say, you went home to a big dinner. Dinner in most families is another social eating oc-casion, and an important one. You weren't hungry, but you ate because the food was there—it looked good, your mother had put a lot of effort into pre-paring it, and everyone else was eating. You may be feeding the social animal, but it is your body that will get fat.

Some groups within our society have a stronger bent toward social overeating than others. Food can be an important part of a culture, as pastas are to Italian-Americans or rice and beans are to Spanish-Americans. Eating such traditional foods can help maintain the social structure of the family and the community by reminding people of their heritage. Even when these foods are no longer economically necessary or physically useful, they are socially sig-nificant, and people are social eaters.

But America's ethnic groups are not alone in their reliance on fattening social foods. The entire mod-ern American diet tends to provide too many calories. Manufacturers and advertisers seem to introduce a new variety of crackers, a new shape in potato chips, a new taste in soda pop almost every day. None of us needs these calorie-filled snacks, but everyone eats them (or at least the ads make us think that everyone eats them) so they are hard to resist, even when our internal signals say "you're full!"

Quick foods—whether from convenient packages or fast-food shops—are all the rage. But these "fun" foods are high in carbohydrate calories and, because of super-processing, they are generally low in food value. Adding such foods to our basic diet puts on weight; filling up with them instead of with more basic foods cheats us of nourishment.

Besides being tempted by a wider variety of fattening food than ever before, we have less need for food than ever before. We are no longer forced to do much of the work that burns up all that fuel. We rely on machines to spend energy: we drive, we phone, we use lawn mowers, washers, and mixers. To burn up the food we take in, we have to seek out exercise—join a gym, or walk when we could more easily ride—and that takes time and effort.

In more primitive societies, where physical labor is necessary to survive, people are rarely fat. The nomadic herdsmen of the deserts of northern Africa and the Near East have adapted to a diet of dairy foods, meats, and some whole grains. What they produce, and it isn't much, they eat. What they eat, their lifestyle easily burns up.

Early Americans needed all the food they ate. Farming, pioneering, building, all took a lot of energy, and our ancestors were lucky that the land was fertile enough to yield the food they required. Hearty breakfasts, big midday meals, and substantial suppers became part of the American pattern of eating. That pattern is no longer useful, but it is still a social habit.

WHEN FAT IS BEAUTIFUL

Society also influences the way you *feel* about fat. The idea that "fat is ugly" is not one that is shared by all the peoples of the world, or even of the United States, today. Fads and fashions have always influenced the way people felt about their figures.

Take a look at a nude painting by one of the great masters—Titian or Rubens, for instance. Art historians and teachers might point out the "glowing flesh tones." But all I can think is, "She's fat! She's even fatter than I've ever been!" But there she is, hanging in all her glory on some famous museum's wall. Why? It's not because whoever painted that fat lady was kinky, it's because, at the time, fat was in fashion.

Many religious idols of Eastern cultures are depicted as fat. In Babylon, Rome, and other ancient civilizations, fat was considered beautiful.

In times and places where food is scarcer than it is in America today, being fat shows that a person is well off. In societies that depend on manual labor rather than on machines, obesity is a mark of status, showing that a person doesn't have to work. Also, where heat is scarce, body fat is needed for warmth.

Among some groups in our own country, the most beautiful woman or handsome man is probably not as slim as a typical model in a national magazine. Spanish-speaking teen-age girls, for instance, are more often worried about being too skinny than too fat.

But people who have been, for better or worse, fully assimilated into modern American culture regard fat as ugly and skinny as beautiful. Now that we are overfed and under-exercised, it seems to be a mark of status to be slender. If you are fat, or think you are, the current fashion puts a lot of pressure on you to kick the eating habit. Whether or not you yield to this pressure is up to you.

FIVE
IS IT ALL IN YOUR HEAD?

Habits are hard to break. But the overeating habit is stronger than others. You know that if you eat too much you gain too much weight. You know that being overweight makes you unhappy. You know that if you eat less you will grow slimmer—and probably happier. And yet you can't eat less. Why?

FAT AS A SYMPTOM

If one morning you broke out in a rash all over your body, you, your family, and your doctor would take that as a symptom, a sign, that something was wrong. You might have measles, or chickenpox. You might have developed an allergy to some food you just ate or some soap you just washed with. The doctor would look at your rash and try to discover what caused it so that he would know how to treat you.

If you suddenly started crying every twenty minutes over "nothing," after a while your parents, your teachers, or hopefully yourself, would see the crying as a symptom of some problem that you might not even be aware of. Commanding you to stop crying would probably do no good. You would need to understand the real cause of the tears in order to stop them.

Just like that rash or those tears, fat can be a symptom, too. We've seen that fat can be a "symptom" of a stage you're going through as your body develops from a child's into an adult's. If you can be patient with yourself, and sensible, you will outgrow the causes of that kind of fat.

We've seen that fat can be a "symptom" of social habits or family custom. If they are the cause for your overweight, the symptom will require slightly more effort to eradicate.

Many people maintain that fat is a symptom of a "weak will." Well, maybe it is, for some people. If you find that simply by exerting "will power" you can avoid eating the foods that make you fat, terrific. But if you can't—if you have all the resolve in the world and still can't lose weight or keep from gaining it—does that mean that you are "weak"? No.

It probably means that your fat, your overeating, are symptoms of forces or feelings that lie deep within you. If you want to lose weight, and keep it off, it will help to understand some of those forces.

You may be *compelled* to eat. A compulsive eater is *not* just someone who eats constantly and can't stop. A compulsion is the irresistible urge to commit an irrational act. Someone who can't resist eating (even an extra cookie a day) when it makes sense not to eat, may be eating out of compulsion. Think about what may compel you to eat. Because you can't get rid of the symptom without understanding and treating the cause.

TRYING TO GET OUT?

"Imprisoned in every fat man is a thin one wildly signalling to be let out." That line by writer Cyril Connolly has been quoted and misquoted many times since he wrote it in the 1940's. It's supposed to give fat people the courage to lose weight.

But is it true? I don't think so, at least for most people. More accurate, I think is one psychiatrist's belief that fat people are *afraid* to be thin. Afraid to be thin? How can that be true, when what you want most in the world is to be skinny. Well, if you want it that much, and you know what to do about it, then why aren't you thin? Some other force—like fear—must be operating to keep you from losing weight.

Let's take a look at how a "fat person" builds up around a "thin person." Sally was thirteen, well padded with the "puppy fat" common to her stage of growth but not obese by any means. She and her friends had been interested in boys for a couple of years, wondering about them from a distance. But then her friends started actually going out with boys and getting involved in a whole new way of life.

Sally envied them, in a way, but she also knew in the pit of her stomach that she wasn't ready for dating. Sally began to draw away from her friends. She spent more time at home, on her own, just sitting around brooding—and eating. So of course, she gained weight. Eventually she was so heavy that no guy would have looked at her even if she had wanted him to. She had saved herself from having to start dating, but she had created a worse problem for herself.

Sally didn't sit down and decide, "I will eat so that I will get fat so that I will be protected against what scares me." She may have felt anxious—that is, afraid of an indefinite something—and her unconscious mind reacted to protect her from this uncomfortable emotion by distracting herself with food. We don't have to be aware of what goes on in our minds and our emotions for them to influence our lives. Sally got fat because she ate more and moved less, but that happened because of her unconscious fears.

Sally was afraid to get thin because she was afraid to start dating and put herself in the position of possible rejection. But why did she choose fatness as her "protection"? She could have gone without bathing or perhaps painted her face green to keep the boys away. Why did her unconscious "choose" overeating? Well, if Sally had used any such bizarre techniques, her parents would have stepped in and stopped the problem. Eating is socially acceptable. It is also a complex and heavily emotional aspect of our lives.

CUDDLING YOURSELF

Think about it. A baby's first important activity outside its mother's body is eating. Its first contact with the world is through its mouth. Its mouth is highly sensitive, and eating is, of course, vitally important to its well-being. When most young babies are fed, they are also held, warmly and comfortably, by someone who loves them and speaks softly to them.

You were a baby, too, and though you probably don't remember these earliest experiences with food, warmth, and mother-love, they remain with you, in your unconscious mind. If your infancy was like most, in the background of your personality is this association between food and comfort. So now, even though you are nearly grown, you still may turn to food when you need some sort of comforting. It can become a substitute for the mother you can no longer snuggle up against.

Adolescence is an anxious, upsetting, and emotional time. One day, or hour, or minute, you may feel giddy with happiness and self-confidence; the next, you may be in the depths of depression and self-doubt. You are excited about the future, but you wish life could be as simple as it used to be.

So, if you eat when you are sad, worried, nervous, afraid, or anxious, you are cuddling yourself. You are trying to recapture that warm, peaceful time you can't consciously remember when someone who loved you held you close and gave you what you wanted. It is a normal feeling, but it makes losing weight difficult unless you understand it.

BABYING THEMSELVES

Your parents, especially your mother, have a stake in those early feeding experiences, too. When you were tiny, the happiest thing your mother could do for you—and herself—was to feed you and snuggle you. Feeding time also shows a mother that the baby is totally dependent on her. She controls its happiness and unhappiness. Even though this isn't such a praiseworthy feeling, it is often there.

For some mothers, these experiences are hard to give up, whether they realize it or not. Let's imagine Sally's mother, for instance. She noticed that Sally was staying home more, eating more, and getting fatter. She could have helped her to lose weight and feel better about herself.

Or, she could have started stocking up on cookies, cakes, and candies, serving richer meals and commenting to Sally about how nice it was to have her around the house for a change. She might not have been consciously aware that she was trying to keep her daughter dependent any more than Sally was aware of why she was overeating. But the effect of Sally's mother was to keep a "baby" around the house.

Now that you are as old as you are, you probably realize that your parents aren't some kind of magical gods. They're people, too, and they have their own fears and worries. They are proud to see you growing up, but they may not like the idea of losing their baby—or of getting old themselves. So without realizing it, they may feed you like a baby.

TAKE A BITE

There are almost as many reasons for overeating as there are fat people. For instance, do you ever eat when you are worried or just plain mad?

When you eat, you bite. Biting, in animals and small children, is a hostile act. It is one way that even the weakest of humans can really hurt someone else. Some people overeat—bite food—because they are angry. They want to attack someone, but they can't, so they attack food instead.

You may be angry at yourself. You may think you should be gorgeous, or brilliant, and you don't think you are. So you punish yourself by biting.

Biting is a good way to strike back at generalized anxiety. If you were afraid of something specific, you would attack it. But anxiety is a nameless fear of something that isn't there. You can't scare it away, so you just bite. And too much biting makes you fat.

TAKE NOTICE

Eating is also a way of getting attention. The little baby who is still lurking somewhere within you noticed very early that when you ate, it pleased your parents. "Ooh, you're such a good baby to finish all your cereal!" Or, food is seen as a reward for being good: "If you behave, I'll give you a lollipop." So if you want to please your parents, to get their attention, or to get proof that you are "good," you eat.

Eating can get attention in more direct ways.

The novel *Dinky Hocker Shoots Smack* offers a good example of how overeating can be a cry for attention. Dinky is a teen-age girl whose mother is so terribly busy with "good works" that she doesn't have time for Dinky. The girl develops an alarming pattern of compulsive eating, and becomes grossly obese.

In part this may have been a way to substitute for her busy mother. But in part, she was saying, "Look at me! I'll get so big you *have* to look at me!"

It's all pretty confusing, isn't it? So now's the time for you to sit quietly and sort out some of the causes, rational and otherwise, for your overeating. Are you afraid of growing up? Are you mad at yourself, your mother, the world? Are you looking for attention? Or what?

By exploring your motives and your feelings, you will get a good idea of what you have to do to lose weight. And you'll have a clearer picture of yourself, too.

SIX
MAKING UP YOUR MIND

Tina was too fat, and she knew it. She had always been a bit pudgy, but when she entered her teens, she began gaining a lot. She knew that people treated her differently because she was fat. She overheard some boys laughing about how brave anyone would be to take "Two-ton Tina" out. The girls were generally nicer to her, but she sensed that they giggled behind her back.

She joined the drama club at school, and was quite a good actress. But she understood perfectly when the coach turned her down for the lead in a play because of her weight.

Angie, her best friend, was loyal, but even Angie had limits. "You know, Teen, I'd like to fix you up with one of Roger's friends, but . . ." Tina knew that what she meant was ". . . but you're so fat." And she accepted that.

Her mother made all her clothes for her, commenting, "You'd never be able to find anything nice-looking that would fit." And Tina felt that her mother was right.

Tina was a smart, sensible, and sensitive girl. If she were honest about it, she could admit that somehow it didn't seem fair that she should be cut off from being considered attractive, from having fun, from aiming for success because of her weight. But she felt she understood the reasons, and she accepted them. That kind of "I-deserve-it" logic only makes a person like Tina fat forever.

"I DESERVE IT"

Psychological tests of overweight teen-age girls have shown that they display attitudes, feelings, and behavior common among members of oppressed minority groups. They feel like outcasts, unworthy of respect, incapable of achievement. After all, girls like Tina *are* discriminated against, and "segregated" from many normal activities just because of a physical characteristic. More disturbing is the report that not only do obese teen-agers feel discriminated against—they feel they *deserve* it.

What about you? Because of your weight, are you excluded, either directly or indirectly, from things you would like to do? If so, do you feel that somehow you deserve it? If you do, why? Answers like, "Well, of course no one wants to date a fatty," or,

"Naturally, they don't make dresses that look good on fat people" aren't good enough. They may be practical responses, but they are superficial. Look deeper.

If you feel that you deserve unfair treatment because you are fat, is it because you see being fat as wicked, and you think justice demands that you be punished? Is it because our society makes such a great thing of being slim that being fat seems to mark you as a failure? Is it because you think so poorly of yourself that it's only right that others do, too?

You need to find any feelings like that and root them out. Because it isn't wicked to be fat. We've seen how complicated overweight is. And if you feel that you deserve to be fat, and to suffer because of your fat, you are not going to be anything *but* fat.

"IT'S HOPELESS"

There's no point in trying to lose weight if you feel it's hopeless. You look at yourself in the mirror and you think, "I'll *never* be able to get rid of all that ugly stuff." Or you compare your weight with the ideal weight on some chart: "Good grief! Twenty pounds too much!" The prospect of losing that much weight is so frightening that you eat a couple of cookies to calm yourself.

Okay, it is depressing and frightening. The idea of dieting may be painful—but it is nothing compared to the idea of being fat for the rest of your life.

One of the reasons you feel that losing weight is hopeless is that you have a rotten opinion of yourself. The same gremlins in your head that tell you you're fat because you're wicked may tell you that you are too "weak" to be anything but fat. That kind of attitude can be a cause or an effect of being fat—or both.

Your body is your own, and so is your mind. If you decide that you want to lose weight, and you think you understand why you are fat and how to get thin, you can do it. No one can stop you.

DO BLONDES REALLY HAVE MORE FUN?

On the other hand, *is* it so awful to be fat? Maybe you've come to the conclusion that being fat wouldn't be so bad if other people didn't make you feel so self-conscious about it.

Your weight is as irrelevant to your competence or your intelligence as your hair color is. And yet not too long ago, ads tried to make us believe that blondes had more fun.

If you're overweight, you probably take a lot of flak about "improving" yourself. That doesn't necessarily mean that your *self* needs fixing, any more than it's true that life is only worth living if you're blonde. It doesn't mean that you must lose weight to be a better person, or to look better, or to "have more fun."

Lots of people in this world are fat, and they don't worry about it. Some are even happy about their weight, or proud of it. Many people just don't think about it—they make the best of themselves and their lives without giving "fat" a moment's consideration. They accept themselves as they are.

Accepting yourself—being satisfied with who you are and how you are—is what counts. Would you be happy to be fat if other people would stop nagging you or teasing you about it? Then try ignoring them and accepting yourself, whatever your weight. Tina's problem, after all, wasn't so much her weight as the way it made her feel about herself.

Of course, strong arguments can be made against being fat. Overweight is bad for your health. And fat literally slows you down. So losing weight does have a point, and you can do it if you want to.

THE RIGHT REASONS

Losing weight depends on dieting for the right reasons. Don't start a diet just because someone else tells you to, even if they may be right. Doctors note that if a parent comes in and says, "I want my child to lose weight," the chances for success are poor.

Your success is important, for your head as well as for your body. You may already feel pretty bad about yourself, and if you let yourself get nagged into a diet without being ready for it, you will probably fail at it. Failure is worse than being fat, because it may reinforce your belief that you are weak and worthless.

Successful dieting means more than just taking off the pounds. It means keeping them off, too. Many fat people go on a diet to punish themselves for being fat, to atone for the "sin" of overeating. Once they have lost the weight, they feel, subconsciously, that they have "paid" for the "crime" of being fat, and they drift back into the habit of overeating. They feel free to commit the offense again. This cycle of repeated binges and crash diets can be dangerous, as it can upset the body's natural balance and put more of a strain on the system than overweight. And it accomplishes nothing.

The right kind of dieting can accomplish a lot. For one thing, it protects your health. Obesity and overweight are linked to heart disease, high blood pressure, and other diseases. Fat can kill you: the likelihood of premature death can increase by almost 50 percent if you are obese. And excess fat can complicate the treatment of almost any illness or injury.

If you get excited only about the effects of overweight right now, go get a suitcase. Gather a stack of books, a pile of rocks or some cans of food that weigh as much as your extra fat, and put them in the case.

Now, try lifting the suitcase. Can you? If you can't, imagine the trouble that your body has carrying around that much extra weight. How far can you carry that suitcase without getting tired, sore, and out of breath? If you can get rid of the excess baggage in your fat cells, you'll be able to walk, bike, dance, swim, have fun without wearing out.

After you've carried that suitcase as far as you can, how much better you feel when you put it down and rest! That gives you an idea of how much better you will feel—how much stronger, lighter, and less tired —after you have lost weight.

You'll feel better in your head, too. You will be proud and happy that you accomplished what you set out to do, with confidence in your ability to do almost anything you want.

SEVEN
WHAT YOU CAN DO ABOUT FAT

You can lose weight, once you really make up your mind to do it. What you need is the right kind of diet for *you*. The right kind of diet is one that is balanced to keep you healthy and sensible and "normal" enough for you to maintain, with some modifications, for a lifetime. In other words, the right kind of diet for you is one that is most easily adapted to your particular eating pattern.

BREAKING THE CYCLE

Why do you overeat? As we've seen, different people have different reasons for it. Only you can answer this question for yourself. Is it because your mother feeds you too much? Why does she, and why do you let her? Is it because you're lonely, or afraid, or mad at the world? Is it because you feel fat anyway, so why not eat? Is it because of all the fun food your friends seem to put away without gaining weight?

When you put your mind to it, you will realize

that your overeating follows a special pattern. Whatever your pattern, you need to understand it to break free. Sit down quietly and privately with paper and pencil and jot down the reasons for your overeating. Just note anything that comes into your head. Put down your reasons for wanting to lose weight, too. And while you're at it, list all the things that make you feel good about yourself. You'll find that one idea will lead to another, until you have a pretty thorough profile of yourself.

You then can carry this brainstorming one step further and start keeping a record of everything you eat, plus when, where, and how you felt at the time you ate it. This kind of record will show what foods you most need to cut out to lose weight. But it will do more. There is little point in trying to eat less unless you understand why you eat. You'll have more success in losing weight if you can change the behavior that *causes* the overeating.

One person's chart looked like this:

MONDAY

Ate	When	Why	How Felt
3 sl. bacon 2 eggs—fried 2 pc. toast & jelly o.j., milk	7.45	b'fast—cooked	hungry

Ate	When	Why	How Felt
doughnut	8:45	J & L stopped at deli	bored
Coke bag pot. chips candy bar	12.30	lunch—everyone there but . . .	wished R. there
strawberry shake	3:15	stopped at Shoppe with J, L, and R	fun
bag of peanuts	3:45	going home alone, R didn't walk w/me	sad & mad
3 glasses gingerale	4–6	homework	bored, restless
meat loaf mashed pot's lima beans cole slaw 2 pc. bread & butter 2 glass milk pc. choc cake	6:30	dinner— cooked	fat
pc. choc cake glass milk	7	doing dishes	mad—not my turn!
2 cans Coke pt. chips	7:30– 9:30	studying for math test	worried
popcorn	9:45	watching TV with Dad	bored, nervous, tired

4 sl. bacon 3 scrambled eggs 3 pc. toast & jelly o.j., milk	7:45	breakfast	nervous— math test
English muffin o.j.	8:15	going over math with J at Shoppe	worried

Keep it handy so you can write down everything you eat, all day, and under what circumstances. Keep the record for a week or so, and then study it. What does it show about your eating habits? Do you tend to skip lunch and then spend your lunch money on snacks with the gang after school? Do you sit around in the evening and nibble in front of the TV because you're bored? Do you take seconds at dinner because your mother makes you feel guilty if you don't? Do you eat a lot because you're nervous before a test? Or because you feel bad about having done poorly on a test? Or because you feel exuberant?

The pattern you see is your own, but for many people the food-and-feeling cycle runs something like this: they eat because they feel angry, or tense, or depressed; the overeating itself, and the fat it puts on, makes them feel even more angry, tense, and depressed, and so they eat more. As this day-today cycle builds into a pattern, they live their lives feeling bad about being fat and eating to make themselves feel better. Whatever your cycle is, the trick is to break it.

CHECKING UP

The next step is to see a doctor. Maybe you can go to your family doctor or clinic on your own, or maybe you have to ask one of your parents to take you. Most parents would be happy to help, but if yours tell you you're just being silly, convince them of your concern. Because you will have to have some kind of medical advice.

It may seem quicker to pick up a diet book or tear a diet plan out of a magazine, or buy diet pills at the drug store, but you're better off in the long run if you see a doctor first. If you've ever tried any of the quickie do-it-yourself methods, you've learned that they don't work, at least not for long, and your eventual failure with them can be a bad blow to your morale.

Pop diets don't teach you a thing about eating right to *keep* the weight off. Besides that, they can be physically harmful to you. An adult has to eat to maintain the status quo, but a person your age is growing. All bodies maintain a delicate balance between intake and outgo, but a body ten to eighteen years old is working on finding the right balance, and it doesn't take much to throw it off.

Let your friends try their own diets, let the magazine writers use their own—your doctor can help you find one that is right for *you*.

Talking your weight worries over with your doctor, your parents, or both, is a good idea for another reason: it gets your feelings out into the open, and when you can be honest about the problem, you can do something about it.

It's possible that you may not be satisfied with your doctor's treatment of you and your problem. Many physicians are too busy or too accustomed to adult patients to devote the necessary time and thought to a teen-ager's special situation. Since the right kind of help is important for your diet and your self-esteem, you may want to seek out a clinic or a doctor specializing in adolescent medicine. Ask your friends and neighbors or inquire at your local medical association. You can also write to the Society for Adolescent Medicine (P.O. Box 3462, Granada Hills, CA, 91344) for the name of the doctor or clinic nearest you.

Once you get to the clinic or doctor's office, what will happen? The doctor will weigh you, measure you, and look you over. He may tell you that you are within the average range for your age and stage and that you have nothing to worry about. Great! But don't leave it at that. If you're concerned about your weight, it's probably because you have more fat than you think you should. Ask the doctor to explain why what you think is "fat" isn't.

Maybe, by talking it over, you'll realize that what you're upset about isn't your weight at all, but something entirely different that you are trying to ignore. You may not be able to resolve conflicts with your parents, or erase anxiety about your future. But the worry has to go somewhere, so rather than face what you're afraid of or can't control, you focus on fat. A bit more exercise and a bit more sleep may be all you need.

If you *are* overweight, the doctor will be able to judge by how much and determine how much it is safe for you to lose and still grow. He may want to run some simple tests to make sure your body is functioning normally. He may ask you to keep a record of the food you eat for a week or so. The chart you've already made may do, or he may want you to count the number of calories and, perhaps, the amount of carbohydrates you take in. He will probably want to know what kinds of exercise you get, and how rapid the weight gain has been.

If the doctor is not too busy, he'll talk with you about how you're doing in school, about how things are going at home, about any special problems or worries you may have. When you're ready for a diet, the doctor will probably want to talk to your parents, too, if only to explain what's happening. This is important, because your family is a big part of your eating pattern. But most doctors say they prefer to do most of the work directly with the dieter. It's the kid's diet, not the parents', and if the parents take responsibility for too much of it, it won't work. Once you start a diet, the doctor will probably ask that you stop in every few weeks to check your progress.

EATING BETTER

If you are ready for a diet, what kind will it be? That is up to you and your doctor. As we've stressed, the diet is only one part of losing weight. Still, after all the psychological probing and self-analysis is through, as a practical matter you lose weight only by taking in less food, burning up more energy, or both.

You may start a *low-calorie diet*. With the doctor, you'll figure out the basic number of calories you need to live and grow. You may also add up how many calories you take in now. You'll need to cut down on the number of calories you eat, but not below the amount you need to maintain activity and health.

A pound of body fat contains 3500 calories of stored energy. If you eat 3500 calories less in a week —or 500 less a day—than you burn, you will lose one pound. The idea is to force your body to burn its extra stores of fat.

There are many ways you can cut out that extra pounds-worth of calories. The doctor may establish a calorie limit for you, within which you can eat almost anything you want. If your eating pattern justifies it, you may be able to avoid the hassle of calorie-counting by simply cutting out calorie-rich but nutrition-poor between-meal snacks. The doctor may put you on a calorie-counting diet that stresses high-protein foods and eliminates most fats and starches.

Some doctors favor, even for teen-agers, a diet that allows the intake of any amount of protein and fat, but prohibits most carbohydrates. In these diets, carbohydrates are measured in grams. Nutritionists recommend the daily intake of no fewer than 100 grams of carbohydrates in a normal diet. A low-carbohydrate diet limits intake to 60 grams daily. And some fad diets try to eliminate them altogether. Since these diets can be very dangerous if not properly followed and understood, they should be started only with a doctor's advice and assistance. The main reason a low-carbohydrate diet is effective is that most of your calories, especially your useless calories, are in the form of carbohydrates. So if you cut down on them, you don't miss many nutrients, but you take in a lot fewer calories.

Any wise diet you start will demand not only that you eat less, but that you eat better. Many fat people are actually undernourished because they fill up on high-calorie junk at the expense of more valuable foods. The chart on page 60 gives the minimum daily requirements for the average teen-age diet.

Proteins are the mainstay of any good reducing diet. They are low in calories compared to carbohydrates and fats and vital to health. Milk and whole-grain breads and cereals provide vital minerals. Fruit and vegetables, even though they do contain sugar and carbohydrates, are necessary for the vitamins and minerals they contain. Fresh fruits are also good substitutes for desserts, and vegetables provide a lot of bulk for an empty stomach. Fats contain the most calories, and on a low-calorie diet they are the first foods to go. For many people, they are the easiest to skip. You can avoid a lot of fat, for instance, if you broil your hamburger rather than fry it, or eat a baked potato topped with broth instead of with butter.

Carbohydrates are easy to avoid, too. You need some breads, cereals and starches but if you skip desserts, or the extra piece of toast in the morning, the candy after school, the potato chips at night,

MINIMUM DAILY REQUIREMENTS
FOR THE AVERAGE TEEN-AGE DIET

Milk and milk products:	Four or more cups of milk or equivalent (1 cup milk = 1 cup yogurt, 1½ cups cottage cheese, 1-inch cube hard cheese, or 2 cups ice cream)
Meat, fish, poultry:	Three 3-ounce servings or equivalent (1 serving = 2 eggs, 1 cup dried beans, or 4 tablespoons peanut butter)
Green and/or yellow vegetables:	Two half-cup servings
Citrus fruits and other vitamin-C sources:	Two servings (1 serving = 6 ounces citrus juice, 8 ounces tomato juice, 1 orange, ½ grapefruit, 1 medium tomato, or 2 cups lemonade)
Bread, cereals:	Four or more servings (1 serving = 1 slice bread, 1 ounce breakfast cereal, or ½–¾ cup pasta)
Butter, oil, margarine:	2–4 tablespoons
Water:	32 ounces
Sweets and sugars:	None required

Source: Deutsch, Ronald M., *The Family Guide to Better Food and Health* (Des Moines: Creative Library, 1971) from the Committee on Foods and Nutrition of the American Medical Association.

you can cut down on calories and still eat your fill with the family.

For some people, a high-protein, low-carbohydrate diet is impractical. You can't very well go home and tell your mother to serve you only poultry, fish, salads and lean meats if the family's menus are built around rice and beans or pork and grits. That's why a doctor is your best guide through the mysteries of dieting. He can help you work out a diet that will take off weight within your own lifestyle. A good diet will be well-balanced, nourishing, interesting, and will help you learn to eat better for the rest of your life.

MOVING MORE

It is possible, of course, to lose weight without eating less—if you exercise more. As you can see from the chart on page 62, you can burn away a lot of that stored energy just by getting out of your chair and moving. When you combine eating less with moving more, you have it made. This combination not only helps you lose weight, but, handled right, it can establish a pattern that will keep you fit forever.

People have some funny ideas about exercise. "It increases your appetite, so you eat more." Well, maybe a fat person uses a walk to the corner as an excuse to eat a sandwich. But actually, regular exer-

ACTIVITY	CALORIES PER HOUR (150-pound person)
sitting	15
standing	20
writing	20
dishwashing	60
walking	
2 mph	200
4 mph	350
dancing	200–400
playing tennis	400–500
rowing (50 strokes/min.)	420
cycling (10 mph)	450
skiing	600–700
swimming (crawl)	700–900
running	800–1000

Source: Mayer, Jean, *Human Nutrition* (Springfield, Ill.: Charles C. Thomas, 1972).

cise may decrease your appetite. By getting your body into the shape it was meant to be in, you restore the balance between intake and outgo, so that the body uses food more efficiently and needs less of it. A fit body also has a greater tolerance of stress, physical and emotional, so strains that once would have sent you to the refrigerator for comfort may not affect you at all.

"Exercise just builds up muscle—it doesn't get you any skinnier." I've noticed that unusually strenuous exercise produces a bloating effect in me, as though unused muscles were taking on a padding of fluid as a protection. But this stage passes. Regular, vigorous exercise does build up muscle. Muscle weighs more than fat, so exercise *can* put on weight. But muscular weight is healthier than fat weight, and a trim body looks better than a flabby one. Your measuring tape will show your progress, even if your scale doesn't. What you're interested in is losing *fat*. What difference does it make how much you weigh? And exercise does burn up stored energy. Check the chart. If you walk for an hour, you can burn up about 350 calories' worth of body fat, and you will weigh that much less.

You may have a different problem about exercise. Some kids get fat because they are too timid to join in the normal play of childhood. You may be so sensitive about the way you look that you shy away from calorie-burning activities like swimming, dancing, or sports. Researchers have observed that even when fat kids do participate in sports, they move less than their normal-weight teammates during the game. If you have been fat most of your life, you've probably not played enough to get the skills necessary for organized games. So you stand back rather than look foolish in competitive play.

But you can get exercise under circumstances that won't make you feel silly. You can do calisthenics or stretching exercises in your room, for instance. Most of these aren't strenuous enough to use many calories, but they can tone you up and trim you down a little—and they make your body feel good.

Some exercises do burn up significant energy. For instance, you can jog in your room. Running uses up about 800 calories an hour. Instead of sitting and munching in front of the TV, try running in place. You're exercising, but the TV keeps you from getting bored. You'll get tired pretty quickly at first, but keep at it for a while. Pretty soon you'll be running through an entire old movie.

Get involved in some noncompetitive exercise. Go swimming at the Y or a local pool, on your own or with a friend. An hour's worth of constant swimming spends about 700 calories.

Join a dance or exercise class. You don't have to feel embarrased about how you look—everyone there is interested in losing weight or inches, too.

Start walking. A brisk stroll to nowhere burns up calories, relaxes you, firms you up, and keeps you away from food. Any errands you can walk on instead of ride takes off that many more ounces and pounds. Can you walk to and from school, or partway there? Try it. If you take a friend along, you'll be surprised at how good and happy you feel.

Ride a bike. Biking is a fast, fun way to get places, and it's good for you too.

Even standing up straight is good exercise—and it makes you look good, too. Stand in front of a mirror as you usually do, then, pull up your chest, pull your shoulders back a bit, and tighten the muscles in your stomach and rear. You are exercising all the muscles you're tightening! To get the feel of standing straight, try pulling your hair: grab a few strands of hair at the crown and tug. Let your body follow the line of least resistance, and you'll find that you are standing straight, without jutting out unnaturally. Hold yourself that way, and you're doing a lot for your looks and your energy balance.

Exercise doesn't necessarily mean playing tennis or working out at a gym. An "exercise program" that will burn calories and get you into great-looking shape follows these rules: *Stand instead of sit, walk instead of ride, run instead of walk.*

EIGHT
WHAT'S WRONG WITH IT?

"LOSE 12 POUNDS IN 2 WEEKS!"

"TAKE OFF INCHES WITHOUT SWEAT!"

"GET SKINNY WITH THIS MAGIC PILL
AND NEVER FEEL HUNGRY!"

Americans spend over $100 million each year on fat cures, and though most of their money is wasted, their hopes are understandable, because the temptations are almost irresistible.

Resist. Anyone who says that you can lose weight without diet or exercise may be out to cheat you. At best, you are going to be disappointed. There is no easy way to lose a significant amount of weight and keep it off. A crash diet of strange foods may work for the short run, but you can't eat bananas or rice exclusively for the rest of your life—so they accomplish nothing worthwhile.

The quickie methods seldom work, and some of them can damage more than your morale. A fad diet that works "miracles" for someone else may be just the wrong one for your system. Most of the diets you can pick up off your newsstand are for adults. Your body is working hard right now, and it needs to be treated with special care.

Even if you do lose weight fast on a miracle diet, the chances are heavily against your keeping it off for very long. You've probably heard that before. Why is it true? It's because being overweight, even by a little, causes your body to adjust the extra load. Your body is used to processing food for a fat person —and recent research indicates that this may be different from the way a slim person's body does. If you lose weight so fast your body can't readjust, it will be hard to restrain yourself from snapping right back into your old habits. Many doctors feel that this "yo-yo" pattern of repeated losses and gains is worse for your health than obesity.

DIET PILLS

The most effective "weight-reducing" pills are *amphetamines*. For many years, doctors prescribed amphetamines for their overweight patients because they suppress the appetite. Scientists don't know why this is so, but they have found that amphetamines work as diet pills only for a short time, and that their side effects, including psychological dependence, outweigh their benefits. As a result, such diet pills have come under strict government regulation, and can no longer legally be passed out in handfuls by obesity specialists—"fat doctors"—trying to make a quick buck.

A doctor may still prescribe "weight-reducing" drugs, even to teen-agers. A wise doctor will not advise amphetamines or other "anti-fat" medicines, especially for a young patient, unless it is an unusual situation for which there is no other solution, and a complete physical examination shows that they will be effective and safe. Not only are most diet pills ineffective after a few weeks, some can cause serious medical problems when used improperly. So beware of them, and don't nag your doctor for some magic pill.

Some "reducing" pills, of course, are available without a doctor's prescription. You can see them, well-advertised, at your drug store. Some of these frankly state that they are diuretics. Diuretics are drugs that cause the body to lose water. When you take them, you spend most of your day in the bathroom, excreting a lot of urine. Diuretics cause you to lose weight because water weighs a lot, but unless you have a heart or kidney problem your body needs this water. And diuretics don't make you lose fat. After a while, they can harm your kidneys and do other damage. Diuretics should only be taken when prescribed by a doctor for people who have specific diseases that cause them to retain too much water.

Other over-the-counter drugs are sold which claim to suppress appetite. Since they cannot legally contain amphetamines, how do they accomplish this? Some of them give you sugar. Sugar does suppress your appetite—by providing calories! Or maybe some of their ads just lie. The government doesn't allow manufacturers or advertisers to lie about their products, but sometimes the legal controls take a while to catch up. The best advice is not to trust any drug that promises to get rid of fat and keep it away.

Researchers are investigating a variety of possible weight-reducing chemicals. One of these, called a "fat mobilizing substance," is derived from the blood of people on fasts. Another is obtained from the urine of pregnant cows or pregnant women. These, or other, reducing aids may be generally available in your lifetime. If so, keep in mind the past histories of other "miracle drugs" and wait until they have been proven effective *and* absolutely safe before trying them. For the time being, there's no such thing as a magic pill to make you slim.

VIBRATORS, SWEAT-PANTS, AND MASSAGERS

When fat pills fell into disfavor, spot-reducing devices and exercise spas came into vogue. You've probably seen their ads on TV and in print. Some swear that if you wear a pair of inflatable pants, an inflatable belt, or a special leotard, you will lose inches where you want to in no time.

The fine print of these ads mentions "special exercises." If you do these "special" exercises, which you could get from any gym teacher or exercise manual, you may indeed firm up your body. The inflatable devices, by causing you to sweat, may make you lose a bit of fluid weight. The special leotard simply imposes extra pull on your muscles, so you have to work harder to exercise. Try doing calisthenics in tight jeans—it will accomplish the same thing, and it costs a lot less.

Some reducing spas offer a diet plan and good hard exercise. There, for a lot of money, you can lose weight and inches. But you can also do this at home, for free. Other reducing spas promise that you can lose size and poundage with "no work." Their machines, they say, do it all. Unfortunately, no machine can shake fat off. No steambath can sweat it off. No masseur can pound it off. These techniques may make you feel virtuous, but they don't make you thin. The only way to lose fat or inches is to exercise and diet.

How can a company promise something that isn't true? Some people believe that anything they read in print, or hear on the air, has to be true. Unfortunately, that isn't so. An honest company will be absolutely truthful about what it promises. Other organizations will tell the truth, but only in the fine print or mumbled speech. And others will just plain lie. Consumer agencies and other government departments will catch up with most of the cheaters, but it takes a while.

LOW-CARBOHYDRATE DIETS

• **WHAT THEY ARE:** Any diet plan that requires you to keep your intake of carbohydrates to less than 60 grams per day is a low-carbohydrate diet. Since an intake of not less than 100 grams a day is recommended for health, you should not undertake such a diet without a doctor's guidance.

In recent years, well-publicized books have promoted a variety of low-carbohydrate diets. Among them are the "calories don't count," the Atkins, the Stillman, and the "drinking man's" diets.

• **HOW THEY WORK:** The average American's diet is overloaded with sweets and starches. By cutting down on these carbohydrates, you also cut out a lot of unnecessary calories, and thus lose weight.

Some doctors limit teen-ager's carbohydrates to 60 grams because this can easily be done by little more than eliminating starchy between-meal snacks. Also, since carbohydrate-counting involves smaller numbers than calorie-counting (see chart, pages 97–101) it is easier to keep track of.

Low-carbohydrate diets not only provide fewer calories than normal eating, they also tend to dehydrate the body, so that the dieter sees a quick loss—but of water, not fat.

Some of the low-carbohydrate diet books stress the *high-protein* aspects of their menus. In theory, a high-protein diet makes weight loss quicker because pure protein stimulates the body to lose more heat than normal, thus forcing the cells to burn extra calories. But there's no food which is pure protein. If you eat only "protein foods" like steak, eggs, or cottage cheese, you also take in fats and carbohydrates, so that the so-called "specific dynamic action" of pure protein is lost. However, in practice, a high-protein diet can reduce you because most "protein foods" are relatively low in calories, and because a growing body needs just about all the protein it can get. So you eat fewer calories, burn all of what you eat, and then lose weight by burning stored fat.

Some low-carbohydrate plans are *high-fat* diets. They claim that you can eat all you want of such "fattening" foods as mayonnaise, cream, or butter and still lose weight without counting calories. And it's true, you can—*but* you must cut your intake of carbohydrates almost to zero. When you do that, you find that there are few "high-fat" foods you can consume, because most such foods—ice cream, nuts, or chocolate, for instance—also contain a lot of carbohydrate. Right away, you've limited the foods you can eat, you have probably limited your calories, and so you lose weight.

If you stick to a high-protein, high-fat, no-carbohydrate diet for a week or more, your body starts to burn vital muscle proteins as a substitute for carbohydrate fuel. Later, stored fat begins to be burned. At this point, substances called *ketone*s are produced. (This type of diet is also called a ketogenic, or ketone-producing, diet.) Ketones in the blood sharply reduce appetite. That way, even though you are allowed to eat "all you want" of high-protein and fatty foods, you don't want to eat much of anything. You eat less, and you lose weight.

• WHAT'S WRONG WITH IT: You need to eat carbohydrates. Without them, the body cannot properly make use of fats, and it must turn to other sources, often all-important muscle proteins, as fuel for energy. Dieters who follow low-carbohydrate plans find that they become cranky and groggy. Without carbohydrate fuel, the muscles work inefficiently. And some evidence indicates that the brain specifically needs a form of carbohydrate for its activities, so without carbohydrates, your thinking and reactions may be impaired.

When you start losing muscle protein, as you do on a ketogenic diet, you can diet yourself into a lot of trouble. You need your muscles, for one thing. For another, the dissolving protein is toxic, or poisonous. The Stillman "water diet" requires the consumption of at least 8 glasses of water a day. This water is absolutely necessary to remove the toxic substances from the blood stream. If they remain, they can cause a form of toxemia, and toxemia is very dangerous. It's a risky proposition at best.

High fat intake is linked to high levels of cholesterol, which can cause heart trouble and other disorders of the circulatory system.

Ketogenic diets, by dehydrating the body, can overwork the kidneys. The ketogenic system also causes the body to produce excess uric acid, which can cause gout, a disease characterized by swollen, painful joints. By following a low-carbohydrate plan for too long, you may lose some weight, but you can seriously damage your health.

More importantly for people your age, a low-carbohydrate diet is nutritionally unbalanced. You may have heard or read about the importance of a "balanced diet." Too many people aren't convinced of this until they have suffered from a continuously *un*balanced diet. Your body is an extraordinarily complicated and delicate machine. Like a machine, it can only function properly on the correct fuel.

Your body is designed to operate on a certain mixture of protein, carbohydrates, and fats. To stay healthy and to grow, you need all these foods, in the right proportions. By cutting out one type, you can't use the others effectively.

Since many necessary foods, like fruits, vegetables, milk products, and whole grains, are high in carbohydrates, if you try to eliminate them because of their carbohydrate count, you also lose out on a lot of essential vitamins and minerals. Vitamin pills can't make up for this loss because many of these "micronutrients" are useful only when you eat them in the context of foods that normally contain them.

An unbalanced diet is not one you can live with permanently. You may lose weight at first, but unless you establish a new, healthy pattern of eating, you'll gain weight as soon as you leave the diet and take up your old habits.

HIGH-CARBOHYDRATE DIETS

• **WHAT THEY ARE**: High-carbohydrate diets eliminate almost all fats and proteins and concentrate on starchy foods. They include the "Kempner rice," the "Rockefeller," the "Zen macrobiotic," and the "inches off" diet. Such plans dropped in popularity in the 1970's, but the fad may return when dieters give up on the no-carbohydrate kick.

• HOW THEY WORK: Most of these plans prescribe what foods, and in what amounts, you can eat. Therefore, they limit the number of calories you take in, so you lose weight. Even when you can eat unlimited quantities, how much rice can you stomach in one day? Probably not enough to make you fat. In addition, by affecting the way the body uses sodium, they cause a loss of water weight.

• WHAT'S WRONG WITH IT: A high-carbohydrate diet is obviously unbalanced. By following it, you miss out on even more important nutrients than on a low-carbohydrate plan. If you stick to it for any length of time, you will get sick. Of course, most of these plans are so dull that you can't stick with them for very long, and when you go off them, you're right back where you started.

"MAGIC FOODS"

• WHAT THEY ARE: Over the years, claims have been made that various foods, such as grapefruit or bananas, help "burn up" fat. So people have tried eating nothing but grapefruit or bananas, and they have lost weight. Other pop diets advocate that you eat ice cream, or candy, or vegetables and almost nothing else. And then there are the all-in-one diet foods like Metrecal and its imitators.

• **HOW THEY WORK**: No food "melts" fat. If you are a sugar-lover and you spend a day eating plain grapefruit, the sour taste in your mouth and the acid feeling in your stomach might make you feel as though you were doing something magic, but you aren't. If you eat only grapefruit, or only bananas, or only vegetables, you're going to take in fewer calories than normal. If you stick to a single-food plan, there's almost no way you can eat too many calories. You can even eat half a pound of butter a day and still lose weight because you will have consumed only 1600 calories.

Of the "magic foods," the Metrecal-type menu is probably the best, because it contains a variety of nutrients. But these formulas make you lose weight only by limiting your daily calorie intake to 900. They don't "burn up" fat.

• **WHAT'S WRONG WITH THEM**: Because a single-food diet is unbalanced, it is unhealthy. It's also boring, so you can't stick with it for long, and after you're through, you still have not developed good eating habits.

STARVATION PLANS

Fasting—eating *nothing*—is a technique people try sometimes. Doctors may put dangerously obese patients in the hospital and feed them nothing but water and vitamins for long periods. Obviously, if you eat nothing, you lose weight. However, you cannot do this for long outside of a hospital without becoming ill. If you've been on an eating binge, you may be tempted to fast for a day or so. This won't kill you, but it won't do you much good, because you'll probably just gorge yourself again after your fast.

There's another kind of "starvation"—psychological starvation. Some poorly planned low-calorie diets have this effect. They are so limited and so boring that you *feel* like you're starving.

With all good intentions, a doctor may suggest a diet plan consisting of menus built around a few specific foods. It may be well balanced, providing for proteins, some fats, leafy greens and other vegetables, and citrus fruits. It may allow exactly the right number of calories for weight reduction and health. But a diet plan, even one that the doctor provides, that offers a week's worth of limited menus to be repeated indefinitely can be boring and discouraging.

"One boiled egg, dry toast, three ounces of poultry, spinach, salad with no dressing, and NO SUBSTITUTES." That kind of plan has given dieting a bad name. You get tired of it, and even if you keep it up long enough to lose weight, you can't stick with it forever—most people don't eat that way.

A WAY THAT WORKS

A better way—one that will keep you slim and healthy for life—is to learn the caloric content and nutritional value of normally available foods and to build interesting menus around them within the calorie and carbohydrate limit you and your doctor have established.

The New York City Health Department devised some interesting and successful weight-reducing plans. The Diet Workshop, Weight Watchers, Inc., and other programs have used diets based on the New York City plan. You'll find information on the Joliffe "prudent diet" and the "New York City diet" on page 104. Basically, they offer menu programs designed to take weight off healthily. Of all the plans available to the general public, these are the most sensible.

Their one drawback is that they tend to make you dependent on a specific pattern of menus and foods. They are fine for taking weight off, but unless you are satisfied with their cuisine, you'll need to reinforce them with your own "plan" if you want to keep slim permanently. That means learning as much as you can about the caloric content and nutritional values of the foods you like, and learning to cook and eat your favorite things for the fewest possible calories.

NINE
PAINKILLERS

Unfortunately, there are no short cuts to losing weight and keeping it off. Here are some ways to make reducing less painful and more efficient.

• DON'T GUESS: Get a *good* calorie book, carbohydrate counter, or both. You'll find a short calorie/carbohydrate chart on pages 97–101, but if possible, get a more complete one. Buy one for your home, and a small one to carry with you. The U.S. Government publishes thorough charts of foods (see page 106). Several paperback books list the calorie and carbohydrate counts of brand-name packaged foods. If you love a certain kind of food you can't find listed anywhere, write the manufacturer for the caloric content and food value.

Learn the values of the foods you eat. You won't have to sit down and memorize them—they'll stick in your mind after you've looked them up a few times.

And learn the energy values of the exercise you take. How many calories do you burn walking to school or riding a bike? Pretty soon, in the back of your mind, a calculator will tick: so much in . . . so much out . . . so many pounds down. It's a good feeling.

• SIZE UP: Get a small kitchen scale, and weigh what you eat. A hamburger can contain 200 or 400 calories, depending on the size, and size is hard to judge, at least at first. Check the sizes of the cups and glasses you use. When a chart says a cup of milk, it means eight ounces, and most glasses are ten ounces or more. Measure your portions. A bowlful of cereal contains more calories than a half-cup full. It's difficult at first, but it's the only way to make a diet work.

• WRITE IT DOWN: Keep thorough, regular, and honest records. Keep a chart in your notebook, pocket, purse, the bathroom, the kitchen—any place that's handy for you and as private as you like. Note every calorie (or carbohydrate gram) you take in, your daily amount of exercise, and your *weekly* weight and measurements.

You might want to include the goal for each week (a pound less by Friday, for instance). But if you don't reach the goal, don't give up. And if you reach or pass it, don't celebrate with an ice cream soda.

• WEIGH IN: A scale is useful, not to compare your weight with others', but to mark your progress. Most experts advise not to weigh daily.

. . . Because on a proper diet you'll be losing weight slowly and you won't see a loss every day, and that can be discouraging.

. . . Because your weight may fluctuate, even if you're sticking to your diet. It can vary according to how much exercise you got one or two days before, or according to how much salt and water you took in. Girls' weights change with the menstrual cycle —many normally accumulate a few pounds of fluid in the week or so before their periods.

. . . Because if the scale shows an increase over yesterday you may get depressed and eat. If it shows a startling decrease, you may be tempted to cheat a little. And daily fluctuations don't count for much.

• USE A SCALE WISELY: No matter how often you weigh yourself, keep these points in mind:

. . . You'll need a good scale—not a super doctor's-office type, but one that doesn't jiggle on an uneven floor or respond sharply to changes in temperature. If it does jiggle, be sure it's always in the same place when you weigh yourself. . . . It doesn't have to be *absolutely* accurate. Since you're using it to show a difference from day to day, it doesn't necessarily have to show your "honest" weight. So what if it says you weigh 160 pounds when the doctor's scale says you weigh 150? As long as it shows you to be 155 after you've lost five pounds, it serves its purpose.

. . . Always weigh at the same time of day and in the same amount of clothing or lack of it. You are apt to weigh the least (and get the biggest morale boost) the first thing in the morning and, if you haven't snacked or had a huge lunch, right before dinner.

. . . Even if you weigh every day, only *record* your weight once a week.

• KEEP LOOKING: In addition to weighing, keep an eye on the mirror and pinch and measure yourself. If you've started an exercise program in connection with your diet, your weight may not go down—it may even go up, briefly—but your measurements may decrease or reapportion themselves, and that's as important as weighing less.

• SET REASONABLE GOALS: You can't lose more than a pound or two a week and stay healthy, so don't promise yourself you'll take off five pounds by Friday and then be disappointed. If the total amount you have to lose seems staggering, break it into chunks and work toward intermediate goals: a quarter of the total in so many months, a half in so many more, and so on.

• BE GOOD TO YOURSELF: Plan non-food rewards for success. When you reach an intermediate goal, get a few new clothes in a smaller size. Don't buy your whole wardrobe till you've lost all you want to. That's expensive. Besides, having your old clothes bag a little is good for your morale. But a new smaller pair of pants or a dress will make you look better and feel proud—and having them a bit snug is a reminder to keep up the good work.

• MAKE ALLIANCES: Enlist your family in the fight. If you're close to your parents, it may help you to confide in them about your progress, your setbacks, your worries and problems. In any case, you'll need some practical help from them: the doctor's visits, fees if you join a diet group, the foods they buy and serve. If they are wise, they'll give you firm support, or at least not try to tear down your efforts to control your eating. If they aren't much help, take the attitude of "I'll show them!"

Watch out for "friendly enemies"—people who say they're with you but actually sabotage your fight against fat. Remember, your family and friends may have a stake in your staying fat. Talk to them about it if you can.

• GET YOUR FRIENDS IN PERSPECTIVE: Heavy kids tend to go around with other heavy kids, and that can fool them into feeling thinner than they are. On the other hand, if all your friends are slim, they may make you feel fatter than you really are. Obviously, you can't cut your friends off just because of your weight or theirs, but you can get them into proper perspective.

Some people make dieting a competitive game or race. If a friend or member of your family has to lose weight, you might have a contest to see who reaches his goal first. But if you are the noncompetitive type, that system may only make you anxious.

Many people of all ages find dieting groups useful. Weight Watchers Inc. is the best known of these, but there are others. Your local Y or other organization may sponsor one. They combine wise dieting with rap sessions and group support to keep you going.

Some summer camps for overweight kids are reported to be excellent. By controlling diet and encouraging exercise, such camps can help a group of people with a shared problem work toward a common goal. Since camps cost money, you'll need your parents' wholehearted support if you are interested. And since camps vary in quality, you'll want to choose carefully. See page 108 for more information about camps.

If a camp or a group is not for you, mark your progress and discuss your hangups with your doctor. And keep looking at yourself and marking your charts.

• IT WON'T ALL BE DOWN: As your doctor will tell you, you may lose weight quickly at first. Some diets are designed to take off the first few pounds quickly. Part of this loss is fluid rather than fat. This kind of progress won't continue, so don't expect it to, and don't be discouraged if after the first couple of weeks the pace is slower.

After you've been on a diet for a while, you'll probably hit a "plateau" as your body readjusts to its new intake levels. This can be discouraging, but stick with it and keep your records well so you *know* you haven't been overeating. Your efforts will show up eventually. The plateau period is a good reason for checking with your doctor or diet group regularly, for reassurance that persistence will pay off.

• WATCH THE BIG PICTURE: It is tempting, when you eat too much in a given day or week to say the heck with it and eat yourself silly. Don't. If you take in 2000 calories too many one day or week, don't compound the error by adding another 2000, simply eat that many fewer over the next few days. If on balance over a week, a month, or a year, your intake is less than your outgo, you will lose weight.

Your diet shouldn't be so rigid that you can't flex it to make up for overeating. If a big eating occasion —birthday, holiday, party, or family gathering—is coming up, prepare yourself by eating much less for a day or two ahead of time. Then you can enjoy yourself without pangs of guilt.

• EAT SLIM: Serve yourself, or have your mother serve you, small measured portions, so you can have seconds (even though they're small) if you want them. If you get a lot on your plate, practice leaving some behind. You'll feel proud of yourself, and your mother may take the hint and start giving you less. Skip dessert, unless it's low in calories, or just eat a few bites.

• EAT SLOWLY: This makes the food last longer, obviously. But you can also feel "full" on less if you eat slowly. Part of the feeling of fullness has to do with the level of sugar in the blood. It takes time for the blood-sugar level to rise enough to affect your appestat. So if you eat slowly, you let your hypothalamus get the message in time to send out a "full" signal before you've gorged yourself. If it's hard to eat slowly, practice counting the number of times you chew each mouthful, or put your fork down between each bite. Wait to swallow one mouthful before taking another.

• DRINK SMART: Some diets recommend not drinking with meals, on the theory that this helps add fluid weight. But if you're used to a glass of something with your meals, it's a hard habit to break. You

might substitute water or diet soda for your meal-
time milk. The fluid will add bulk to a low-calorie
meal without adding calories. Save your milk allot-
ment for a snack or cooking. A big glass of water, a
cup of bouillon, or a small glass of tomato juice
before a meal can keep you from feeling ravenous
when you sit down at the table.

• SWITCH THE SALT: Salt your food less. This will
help keep off water poundage. It's also a good practice for a lifetime of eating, because we all get
plenty of salt in cooked and prepared foods, and too
much additional salt can be unhealthy. Your doctor
may tell you to cut out salt completely, and you'll
need to find some flavor substitutes. If not, put your
salt in a pepper shaker to get less salt with as many
shakes. Put your pepper in the salt shaker—pepper
adds a lot of zip without holding water.

• SALT AND WATER MIX TOO WELL: Some dieters believe that if they drink any water at all, they will
add "water weight." Some fad diets recommend
drinking enormous quantities of water, on the
theory that somehow it will "wash away fat." Neither
idea is true.

Here are the facts. A teaspoon of salt helps your
body retain a pint of water. And a pint of water
weighs a pound. So if you oversalt your foods, or
eat a lot of salty foods—ham, potato chips, salted

peanuts, Chinese food with extra soy sauce—your body will hang onto a lot of water.

This does not mean that you should cut out salt or water entirely. Your doctor will tell you if you should cut down radically on your salt intake, but otherwise, just go a little easy with the salt shaker to avoid demoralizing bloating. Your body does need salt for health.

Your body needs water, too. Not gallons of it—it doesn't "wash away" fat. But water keeps the system flowing properly. Your kidneys, for instance, are responsible for much of the waste-removal in your body. Your kidneys need water to function. If they get too little, fluid waste will back up in the system and cause bloating just as salty water does.

Four glasses of water (in *addition* to milk, juice, soda or other liquids) are about the right amount. Does that sound like a lot to you? It doesn't take much getting used to, and it is important, for your health and your diet, to get enough water. To get in practice, drink a glass of water after every trip to the bathroom. Drink a glassful before meals. Pretty soon, your body will crave water, and you'll get thirsty enough to drink the right amount without thinking. Water keeps your stomach and mouth busy, with no calories. Try it *hot* sometime. Hot water with a few drops of lemon juice may sound yukky, but give it a try. It warms you up, tastes surprisingly good, and even seems to satisfy hunger, all without adding an ounce of fat. It can help take care of the constipation some dieters suffer, too.

• IT WON'T GO UP IN SMOKE: You may have read that people who stop smoking gain weight, and you may be tempted to light up instead of eating. Smoking will not help you lose weight. People who get fat after quitting do so because they eat more to keep their mouths busy. There's no such thing as smoking for the duration of a diet and then giving it up.

• LEARN WHAT'S COOKING: Find out about low-calorie cooking and diet substitutes for fattening foods. You can't demand that your mother serve you lean meats and salads if the family's diet is heavy with fats and carbohydrates. But you can clue the cook in your household in on low-calorie cooking. Better yet, do it yourself. You may already handle at least some of the cooking and shopping for your family. If not, this is a good time to start. What better way to convince your mother that you're serious, and make her feel good about your diet?

Get a good low-calorie cookbook (see page 107) and remember these general rules:

- Broiled foods contain fewer calories than fried or roasted.
- You don't need to add butter or oil to every-

thing you cook. Let the non-dieters add these at the table.

- Low-cal dressing or oil-and-vinegar that's mostly vinegar is best for salads—or let everyone dress his own at the table.
- Drain all meats after cooking. If you broil chopped meat and drain it on paper towels before adding it to casseroles, chili, or spaghetti sauce, you lose most of the fat and save lots of calories while still being able to eat these "rich" foods.
- Cut *all* visible fat off the meats you cook and eat. You can eat much more trimmed meat than untrimmed for the same calories. Skip the skin on chicken or turkey—that's where the fat is on poultry.
  Cook with non-stick pans, or use well-"seasoned" cast iron pans that need only a wipe of oily paper to keep foods from sticking.
- You can make full-sized but low-calorie sandwiches if you halve thick slices of bread (it's tricky, but worth it if thin-sliced loaves aren't available) or scoop out the fluffy insides of hard rolls—you'll feel like you're eating bread, but you're avoiding most of the calories.
- Experiment with seasonings. Herbs and bouillons contain almost no calories but can make foods taste great.

- Find new ways to cook your favorite foods. Potatoes, for instance, needn't be skipped on a low-calorie diet as long as they aren't topped with butter or sour cream (try replacing the sour cream with yogurt for a lot less fat). Bake one, halve it, and fluff up the insides with a bit of broth. . . . Baked potato slices go a long way and taste great: oil the outside of a clean potato, slice it thin, salt and bake the slices, covered, for twenty minutes at 375°. This way, one good-sized potato can serve four people, and it tastes terrific. . . . If you have a blender, follow the standard blender recipe for mayonnaise, but instead of adding a full cup of oil for each egg, stop pouring in oil as soon as the mixture thickens—about half the cup of oil. You'll have about half the calories, and the result tastes as good as the off-limits variety.

If you take over some of the cooking, you'll have a lot of fun without gaining weight.

- HOW TO CHEAT: Make use of the low-cal foods on the market. This kind of cheating is fair, as long as you remember that the originals you get in the snack shop aren't "dietetic."

- Drink diet soda instead of regular. There are so many kinds you're sure to find one you like.

- Buy whipped butter, margarine, or cream cheese for the same amount with fewer calories.
- Use low-calorie salad dressings, gelatins, puddings, toppings.
- Learn the many ways in which yogurt can add variety and rich taste to a low-calorie diet. (The types mixed with preserves are rather calorific, but the vanilla and coffee flavors aren't so bad— or sweeten plain yogurt with sugar substitutes or mix it with fresh or diet-packed fruit.) Yogurt and onion-soup mix or other seasonings makes a great dip. Combine yogurt with low-cal gelatin for puddings or parfaits that are practically weightless. And frozen yogurt tastes like ice cream but has fewer calories.
- Get tuna packed in water instead of oil, and canned fruits packed in water or juice instead of syrup.
- Buy or learn to make sponge cakes and angel-food cakes. They have fewer calories than rich pastries.
- Switch to skim milk (unless you're counting only carbohydrates). Some people find they like it better than whole milk. If you don't, mix your milk half-whole and half-skim for some of the flavor with less of the fat.

- READ LABELS CAREFULLY: Any food that claims in any way to be "low-calorie" or "dietetic" *must* list

the caloric content on the label. If it doesn't, skip it
—and write a letter to your consumer bureau. You
may find that some foods that call themselves "diet"
have no fewer calories—but a higher price—than
regular products.

Some "dietetic" foods are intended for diabetics
or for people who must follow a low-salt diet. They
usually have no fewer calories than other foods.
Many "dietetic" candies, for instance, contain less
sugar, but no fewer calories than regular. They have
the same number of calories per *pound,* but fewer
per *piece,* because the pieces are smaller. You're
probably better off checking the calorie book for
low-calorie regular candy.

Ice milk, "low-fat" yogurt and cottage cheese, and
dry-roasted nuts do *not* contain significantly fewer
calories than regular ice cream, yogurt, cheese, or
nuts. They simply have less fat. And if you're counting only carbohydrates, they're worse for your diet
than the standard varieties.

• GET SET FOR SNACKS: Make sure you have lots of
low-calorie snacks ready and waiting. Store celery
and carrot sticks in ice water in the refrigerator.
Keep a supply of small fruits. Keep ready-cut and
pre-measured cubes of cheese or cold cuts in plastic
bags. Have *small* and crunchy crackers and eat
them one at a time. Bouillon and tomato juice fill
you up for few calories. Some frozen treats, like pop-

sicles, give a lot of pleasure for not many calories, or you can make your own by freezing lo-cal syrup mixed with water. If you like nuts, buy them in the shell, so you'll have to work hard to get a few instead of grabbing up a handful of calories.

• TIRED, HUNGRY, AND COLD? For many fat people, hunger is a strange feeling. If you don't like that feeling, tighten your belt, literally. That's a technique poor people have used for generations, and it works: a tighter belt makes your stomach feel fuller (but don't go to extremes—you can clog yourself up if it's *too* tight!).

We burn more calories when it's cold, as the body works harder to maintain temperature. By lowering the thermostat, you might use up a bit more stored energy. It's not much, but every little bit helps.

Eating less may make you tired, at least at first. It gives some people a headache. If you're tired, lie down. If you get a headache every now and then, take an aspirin.

• BALANCING OUT: After you've worked at your diet for a while, you'll get a feel for your own intake-outgo balance. You'll learn to pay attention to your body and its needs. It's a sense you won't lose.

• PLAN TO STOP: Sometimes people get so involved with a diet that they can't quit even when they have lost enough weight. Others return to their normal calorie level so abruptly that their weight bounces up maddeningly. So, when you approach your weight goal, keep using your head. You may want to go a few pounds below your desired weight, so that your body has room to readjust to more normal eating. Add calories gradually, over a few days or weeks, until you've reached the limit that will keep your intake and outgo in balance permanently.

• JUST LOOK AT YOURSELF: By the time you're well into your diet, you ought to know yourself pretty well. Keep in touch with your feelings, and learn to deal with them directly. If you're angry, don't eat—get mad. Tell someone off or go to your room and scream and throw pillows. If you're depressed, cry if you want to. Try to figure out what's wrong and straighten it out. If you're tense, take a walk. Food solves no problem but malnutrition. Once you realize that and can face yourself honestly, inside and out, you'll be a person you're happy to live with.

CALORIE-CARBOHYDRATE CHART

This chart is not intended to be complete. Rather, it is included to give you an idea of the calorie and carbohydrate values of a few common foods. You should do everything possible to get a good calorie and carbohydrate counter (see page 106).

Food	Amount	Calories	Carbo-hydrates
MEATS AND FISH			
beef			
hamburger, broiled			
lean	4 ozs.	248	0
regular	4 ozs.	324	0
steak, broiled			
lean and fat	4 ozs.	463	0
lean only	4 ozs.	245	0
bologna	½-oz. slice	36	.5
chicken, broiled	4 ozs. (no skin)	154	0
fish			
bluefish, baked	3 ozs.	135	0
fishsticks, breaded	10 sticks	400	15
swordfish, broiled	3 ozs.	150	0
tuna, canned in oil	3 ozs. drained	170	0
lamb, roast			
lean and fat	4 ozs.	316	0
lean only	4 ozs.	211	0

Food	Amount	Calories	Carbo-hydrates
pork			
bacon, crisp	2 thin slices	90	1
fresh, roasted			
lean and fat	4 ozs.	400	0
lean only	4 ozs.	277	0
ham			
lean and fat	4 ozs.	424	0
lean only	4 ozs.	246	0
veal cutlet, broiled	3 ozs.	185	0

DAIRY PRODUCTS

Food	Amount	Calories	Carbo-hydrates
butter	1 tablespoon	100	.1
cheese			
cheddar	1" cube	70	.4
cottage			
creamed	1 cup	260	7
uncreamed	1 cup	170	5
Swiss	1" cube	55	.5
cream, light	1 tablespoon	30	1
eggs			
boiled	1 large	81	.4
fried in fat	1 large	99	.1
scrambled, milk & fat	1 large	110	1
ice cream, plain	1 cup	255	28
ice milk	1 cup	200	29
milk			
skim	1 cup	90	12
whole	1 cup	160	12
milkshake	1 cup	apx. 275	apx. 38
yogurt, plain	8 ozs.	136	14
coffee & vanilla	8 ozs.	198	33
mixed with preserves	8 ozs.	apx. 260	apx. 51

Food	Amount	Calories	Carbo-hydrates
VEGETABLES			
asparagus	4 spears	10	2
beans			
green	½ cup	15	5
lima	½ cup	95	17
cabbage, raw	½ cup	10	2.5
carrots, raw	1	20	5
celery	2 large stalks	10	4
lettuce	2 large leaves	10	2
peas, cooked	½ cup	58	9.5
potato			
baked	1 medium	90	21
french fried	10 pieces	155	20
tomato	3″ diameter	40	9
FRUITS			
apple	1 medium	70	18
banana	1 medium	100	26
blueberries	½ cup	43	10.5
cantaloupe	½ melon	60	14
grapefruit	½ medium	45	12
orange	1	65	16
peach	1 medium	35	10
pear	1	100	25
strawberries			
fresh	½ cup	27	6
frozen with sugar	½ cup	162	39
watermelon	1 wedge 4″ × 8″	115	27

Food	Amount	Calories	Carbo-hydrates
BREADS AND STARCHES			
bread			
white, soft	1 reg. slice	70	13
	1 thin slice	55	10
whole wheat	1 reg. slice	56	11
doughnut	1	125	16
macaroni			
cooked 8–10 min.	1 cup	192	39.1
cooked 14–20 min.	1 cup	155	32.2
pancake	1, 4"	60	9
pizza, cheese	⅛ of 14" pie	185	27
rice, white	½ cup	112	25
roll			
hamburger, hot dog	1	120	21
hard	1	155	32
spaghetti			
cooked 8–10 min.	1 cup	216	43.9
cooked 14–20 min.	1 cup	155	32.2
SWEETS AND DESSERTS			
cake			
angelfood	1/12 of 8" cake	108	24.1
chocolate layer	1/16 of 10" cake	443	67
plain with icing	1/16 of 10" cake	368	59
candy			
chocolate bar	1 oz.	152	15.9
hard	1 oz.	110	26
jelly beans	1 oz.	90	25
licorice	1 oz.	100	25
cookie, chocolate chip	1	50	7
honey	1 tablespoon	65	17

Food	Amount	Calories	Carbohydrates
jam or jelly	1 tablespoon	50	13
maple syrup	1 tablespoon	50	13
pies, 2 crust	1/7 of 9" pie	apx. 350	apx. 50
sugar	1 tablespoon	40	11

SNACKS

corn chips	1 oz.	164	15.2
crackers			
cheese-sandwich	1 pack	209	22.7
saltines	4	48	7.9
soda	2	48	7.8
peanut butter	1 tablespoon	93	2.8
peanuts, shelled	1 oz.	165	5.8
popcorn			
plain	1 cup	23	4.6
w/oil, butter	1 cup	41	5.3
potato chips	10 chips	114	10
soft drinks			
cola	6 ozs.	73	18.5
ginger ale	6 ozs.	64	16.5

OILS AND DRESSINGS

French dressing	1 tablespoon	65	3
ketchup	1 tablespoon	19	4.6
margarine	1 tablespoon	100	.1
mayonnaise	1 tablespoon	100	.3
mustard	1 teaspoon	8	.5
salad oil	1 tablespoon	125	0

Sources: U.S. Department of Agriculture, *Composition of Foods* (Washington, D.C.: U.S. Government Printing Office). Barbara Kraus, *Calories and Carbohydrates* (New York: Signet Books, 1973).

WHERE TO FIND OUT MORE

Check these books for more facts about fat and fighting it. If you can't find them at a bookstore, you can order them from the publishers or borrow them from the library.

BOOKS ABOUT DIETING AND DIETS

Berland, Theodore, and the Editors of *Consumer Guide*, *Rating the Diets* (Skokie, Illinois: Publications International, 1974).

> A quick look at the causes for fatness and a sensible summary of nutritional needs, good and bad diets, and a good section on exercise. Available from Consumer Guide, 3323 W. Main Street, Skokie, Illinois 70076.

David, Lester, *Slimming for Teenagers* (New York: Pocket Books, 1966).

> This short book is a bit out of date and somewhat superficial, but its dieting advice is sound and recommended by the American Medical Association. It may be available at your library.

Guilford, Carol, *The Diet Book* (New York: Pinnacle Books, 1973).

> Summary and description, with some judgments, of some of the most popular fad diets, plus a miscellane-

ous collection of other dieting information and a large
bibliography.

Joliffe, Norman, *Reduce and Stay Reduced on the Prudent
Diet* (New York: Simon and Schuster, 1963).
> The author, a nutrition expert, designed this well-
> balanced, low-fat, long-term diet primarily for adults.
> A good, safe guide nonetheless.

New York City Health Department, *Eat to Lose Weight*.
> An effective, sensible plan. Available *free* from Bureau
> of Nutrition, Dept. of Health, 93 Worth Street, New
> York, New York 10013.

Rubin, Dr. Theodore I., *The Thin Book by a Formerly Fat
Psychiatrist* (New York: Simon and Schuster, 1967).
> Dr. Rubin works with fat people, among others, and
> has first-hand experience with dieting. His book is
> addressed to adults, especially men, but it's full of
> interesting ideas and encouragement for dieters of
> any age.

United States Department of Agriculture, *Food and Your
Weight* (Bulletin G 74) (Washington, D.C.: U.S. Government Printing Office).
> An introduction to weight-control, dieting, and calorie-
> counting. Available *free* from the Office of Informa-
> tion, U.S. Department of Agriculture, Washington,
> D.C. 20250. Be sure to include your name, address,
> and zip code.

West, Ruth, *The Teen-Age Diet Book* (New York: Julian
Messner, 1969).
> This is a revision of an earlier book that was once
> available in paperback. Even in hardback, the ideas
> are good, and the recipes are great! (See Cookbooks,
> below.)

BOOKS ABOUT EXERCISE

Lettvin, Maggie, *The Beautiful Machine* (New York: Alfred A. Knopf, 1972).

> The most effective set of exercises I have ever tried (and I've sweated through a lot of them). The "book" is a collection of cards illustrating and explaining 180 exercises, plus a pamphlet-sized planning guide. It isn't cheap, but it's a bargain. In addition to lots of trimming-down and building-up routines, there are exercises for use during pregnancy, after injury or illness, and in old age, so the price is a long-term investment. Or, you can share the cost with a friend and split the cards.

The President's Council on Physical Fitness and Sports, *Vigor* (Washington, D.C.: U.S. Government Printing Office).

> A guide to exercise and fitness for boys.

Prudden, Bonnie, *Teenage Fitness* (New York: Harper & Row, 1965).

> An exercise expert offers advice and instruction for a sensible personal fitness program.

BOOKS ABOUT FEELINGS

Rubin, Dr. Theodore I., *The Angry Book* (New York: Macmillan, 1969).

——, *Winner's Notebook* (New York: Trident Press, 1967).
> This "formerly fat" psychiatrist provides some easy-to-read suggestions for sorting out your feelings instead of turning them into fat and other disabilities.

BOOKS ABOUT NUTRITION

Deutsch, Ronald M., *The Family Guide to Better Food and Better Health* (Des Moines, Iowa: Better Homes & Gardens, 1971).

> A clearly written, complete guide by a noted nutritionist, if you want to know a lot about the way your body works and what's in the foods you eat.

Salmon, Margaret B., *Food Facts for Teenagers* (Springfield, Illinois: Charles C. Thomas, 1965).

> An easy-to-read guide to nutrition.

CALORIE-COUNTING BOOKS

Kraus, Barbara, *Calories and Carbohydrates* (New York: New American Library, 1973).

> This seems to be the most complete and most accurate handbook of the calorie and carbohydrate content of foods currently available. It includes counts for brand-name products as well as basic foods.

United States Department of Agriculture, *Calories and Weight* (Washington, D.C.: U.S. Government Printing Office).

> This is the Department of Agriculture's pocket-sized calorie guide. Available *free* from the Department.

——, *Composition of Foods* (Handbook #8) (Washington, D.C.: U.S. Government Printing Office).

> This publication lists the food values and caloric content of over 2400 foods (many of which you'd probably never think of eating). Though it's a bit hard to use and perhaps gives more information than you want to know, it is *the* source for complete information about the foods we eat. Available from the U.S. Government Printing Office, Washington, D.C. 20402.

———, *Nutritive Value of Foods* (Washington, D.C.: U.S. Government Printing Office).

> This is a condensed version of the *Composition of Foods*, not as complete but just as accurate, and easier to handle. Available *free* from the Department.

DIET COOKBOOKS

Nidetch, Jean, *The Weight Watchers Program Cookbook* (Great Neck, New York: Hearthside Press, 1972).

> Good ideas for tasty, non-fattening foods. Caloric counts *not* included.

West, Ruth, *The Teen-Age Diet Book* (New York: Julian Messner, 1969).

> This overall diet book has some excellent recipes for low-calorie versions of the kinds of foods you like to eat. I've used them for years.

You'll find many other diet cookbooks in your bookstore and library, and most of them are good. In choosing them, be sure that they are for general reducing diets and not specialized ones (such as low-sodium, diabetic, or the like). They should be well detailed and give the caloric content of measured portions. Many magazines often run sections on diet recipes. Keep your eye out for them. Just make sure they are *really* low-calorie. Sometimes they provide for portions so tiny, only a fly would enjoy them.

NOVELS WITH FAT AS A THEME

Hamilton, Virginia, *The Planet of Junior Brown* (New York: Macmillan, 1971).

> A talented fat boy lives in a fantasy world.

Irwin, Ann, *One Bite at a Time* (New York: Franklin Watts, 1973).

> A fat girl learns to value herself.

Kerr, M. E., *Dinky Hocker Shoots Smack* (New York: Harper & Row, 1972).

> Dinky eats to get attention, and when she gets it, she starts unraveling some of her problems.

Orgel, Doris, *Next Door to Xanadu* (New York: Harper & Row, 1969).

> For "Fatsy Patsy," food is her only friend, until she finds a better one.

Perl, Lila, *Me and Fat Glenda* (New York: Seabury Press, 1972).

> A girl from an eccentric family forms a strong friendship with Glenda because they both understand what it means to be a "freak."

FOR FURTHER HELP

You can get special information and advice about weight and health from the following organizations:

American Camping Association
Bradford Woods
Martinsville, Indiana 46151

> The association sells a directory to all types of camps. Unfortunately, the diet and exercise programs at weight-reducing camps are not evaluated.

Diet Workshop, Inc.
28 Merrick Ave.
Merrick, New York 11566

> A group that provides rap sessions and personalized diets for moderate fees through franchises across the country. Its special advantage is that, instead of for-

bidding certain foods forever, it shows members how to eat and cook most foods for the least calories.

TOPS
4575 South Fifth Street
P.O. Box 4489
Milwaukee, Wisconsin 53207

"TOPS" stands for "Take Off Pounds (Sensibly)." Chapters around the country provide counseling, rap sessions, information, and other services in return for very small yearly fees. The group's goal is to help its members stick with the diets their own doctors have prescribed. Some chapters have teen-age sections.

Weight Watchers International, Inc.
(check phone book for nearest franchise)

This well-publicized, profit-making organization provides the same sort of services as TOPS and Diet Workshop, but for higher fees. It requires members to follow a specific diet.

In addition to these action programs, quite a bit of general information on weight control and health is free for the asking, if you know where to ask. Here are some good sources:

U.S. Government:

Office of Information
U.S. Department of Agriculture
Washington, D.C. 20250

U.S. Department of Health, Education, and Welfare
Washington, D.C. 20201

President's Council on Physical Fitness and Sports
Washington, D.C. 20201

State and Local Governments:

Address the department of health, in care of your city hall or state capitol (include the zip code).

INDEX

scientific description of, 14–15

Flab, 12. *See also* Fat

Foods: burning, 15–16; categories of, 16–17; chemical composition of, 15–16; dietetic, 93–94; quick, 31; supplying carbohydrates, 17, 19, 75; supplying fats, 17, 19–20; supplying protein, 16

Frame. *See* Bone structure

Friends, influence of, 84–85

Genes, 21

Goals, in dieting, 83

Habit, 29–31. *See also* Eating habits

Health spas, 69–70

Heat, body, 17

Heredity: and fat cell formation, 21; as factor in weight gain, 25–26

High-carbohydrate diets: dangers of, 76; described, 75–76; types of, 75

High-fat diets: dangers of, 73–75; described, 18, 72–73

High-protein diets: dangers of, 73–75; described, 72

Hormones: insulin, 22; production of, during puberty, 8–9

Hunger pangs, 28

Hypothalamus, 28–29

Infants: fat cell formation in, 21–22; parental attitudes about feeding, 39–40

Instinct, and eating, 27–28

Insulin, 22

Joliffe diet, 79

Kempner diet, 75–76

Ketogenic diets, 73–74. *See also* Low-carbohydrate diets

Ketones, 73

Kidneys, 89

Lipid, 14

Losing weight. *See* Dieting

Low-calorie diet, 18, 57–58

Low-calorie foods, 93–94

Low-carbohydrate diets: dangers of, 73–75; described, 18, 58–59, 71–73; types of, 71

Macrobiotic diets, Zen, 75

Massage, 69–70

Medical supervision, and dieting, 12, 54–58, 61, 67–68

Menu preparation, 90–93

Metabolism, 15

Metabolism rates, 24

Metrecal diet, 76–77

Minerals, 19, 59

Minimum daily requirements, for teenagers, 60